Echoes of Jerry

by
Judah Leblang

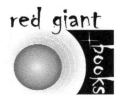

red giant
books

Dedication

To Helene, who believed I had a story to tell and the ability to tell it,

to my mother, who instilled her love of books in her middle son,

to my uncle and grandparents, who bequeathed this story to me,

and to Russell.

Table of Contents

Part Three: Finding Jerry and Myself

Prologue

The postcard sits on my cherry-wood desk, a reminder from my audiologist's office; the warranty on my hearing aid is about to expire and I must come in for service. Looking at the card, I feel defective like my first car, a 1968 Chevrolet Corvair, "unsafe at any speed."

At 50, I was yanked back into the world of hearing loss, specialists, and assistive devices. I tried three different aids to finally find one that amplified speech without excessive noise, though it never worked particularly well. I'm a man who suddenly lost most of the hearing in his left ear for no known reason. Over the last few years, I've reached an uneasy peace with the aid, still longing for my hearing to return.

But I was too afraid to find out. Until now. The aid was due for a check-up, and so was I. Now I sit in a soundproof booth, looking through glass at my audiologist Rachel, a Southern blonde, as she fiddles with the controls on a large console. I sit in the closed, silent space, sweat trickling down my neck despite the refrigerated air, headphones clamped around my ears, while I strain to catch a series of beeps just beyond my reach. The hearing test drags on. My stomach tightens like a fist; I realize I'm not breathing. A wave of white noise, annoyingly loud—SSSSHHH—cascades in my right ear, drowning out the words in my left. The test measures my ability to decipher speech through background noise — the reality of my life today. My skin burns as I listen.

"I'm done," I tell the audiologist through the glass, reaching for the clammy headphones. "We're almost finished," she says through speakers. I already know the verdict; soon she makes it official. My bad ear has gotten worse.

"There's always surgery," she says. My conductive hearing loss, which is located primarily in my middle ear, might be improved by surgery. Or I could wind up totally deaf in one ear.

"I can't think about that right now," I say.

Soon I will return to get the aid adjusted, to try (and ultimately fail) to recapture the volume I have lost. My hearing will never again be normal. I must adjust to the new reality and my dependence on this small instrument. It is both a poor substitute for what has gone away and a link to my Uncle Jerry, another in a long line of echoes that continues today, four decades after his death.

Part One
Things Fall Apart

Chapter 1

A Family Affair

The house was strangely quiet that first week of May 1975, as if time were suspended. Looking back, perhaps it was during that brief window, after I learned of my father's affair, and before Uncle Jerry died.

On the wall of my mother's gilt wrapped kitchen—the gaudy wallpaper her attempt to pull our '60s style colonial into the mid-1970s—was a 10x12-inch poster created by my brother Alex, to mark my parents' 25th wedding anniversary. The card was sweet and simple, a reflection of my brother and his quiet but sunny temperament. On the white poster were the words Happy Anniversary below the number '25' laid out in quarters, a considerable sum for a 12-year-old. Above those quarters was a small picture taken the year before, the happy couple seated in their usual pose—Dad left, Mom right, their heads almost touching, their connection palpable.

Now the picture seemed ironic, a sad commentary on the past few months, a time of angry standoffs, slamming doors, of voices raised in other rooms. I did my best to ignore it, to pretend (as they did) in the public spaces of our kitchen, family room, and my father's den, that everything was fine, normal, OK.

I watched myself, suddenly self-conscious around my Dad, armed with my newfound knowledge that he was "carrying on" with a younger woman, that he was distant from my mother and now—without his knowledge—from me. The house felt colder than usual that spring, the sniping between my parents seeping out from behind closed doors like a toxic cloud.

They were away, together, for a Mexican vacation—a break in the action. Perhaps they would return in better moods. Perhaps it would all work out. But I doubted it; I'd inherited or imbibed my mother's worldview, which was reinforced by a series of accidents, and which led me to view life as a series of dangerous events, best (but impossible to) avoid.

Now, with just Alex and Donna, our maid, holding down the fort, I could breathe and think about my upcoming graduation and the summer to come, which stretched out before me, endless. I saw my way out on the other side of that summer, and wished for it to hurry by, as if I could speed the passage of time through will alone. It was just a few days into that week when I walked into the cool stillness of our back hallway and learned that my only uncle had died.

Chapter 2

The Price of Silence

My parents rushed home. Arrangements were made and shiva was set at Nanny Fay and Papa Ben's house. It felt surreal; Jerry had always seemed so powerful, an ex-high school jock who played a bit too rough, who expressed physically what he couldn't say in words. When I was six, eight or ten, he lifted me to the ceiling, tickling me as I rose toward the lights. Now his heart had betrayed him, as his ears had done years before.

•

I sat in Arthur Treacher's Fish and Chips on a rainy Sunday in 1972, a fifteen-year-old boy staring through glass at the brick edifice of Cleveland Heights High School across the street. The smell of hot grease permeated the fast-food restaurant, adding to the general gloom. As Papa Ben talked with my mother, Uncle Jerry squeezed my shoulder and pointed across to the schoolyard.

"I played basketball and ran track—got varsity letters, you know? Only deaf kid in the whole league." Jerry's index finger tapped his broad chest, and I saw his eyes go back there, to high school in the early '50s. His words pelted me like the rain outside, his vowels flat and hard. I nodded, impressed, and knew I'd never earn a high school letter. My best sports were tetherball and ping-pong.

I envied Jerry for his athletic prowess, but why he did he still live in his memories of twenty-odd years ago? He was staying with Nanny and Papa again, back home after ten years of marriage. His deaf wife, my Aunt Terri, had left him and moved back to Illinois with their hearing daughter, Sue. Jerry had no hobbies that I knew of other than watching Cleveland Browns football and pro wrestling on TV and dancing. My uncle loved to dance.

My grandfather called out and told me to nudge Jerry, to get his attention. Soon I heard Papa Ben's familiar refrain when he rasped, "How many times have I explained all this, how many times have I told you this before?" as he lectured my uncle about being a responsible adult.

The specifics were lost on me; I tuned out Papa's voice and focused on his face, which had turned from taupe to rose. Papa's scruffy mustache obscured his lips and a vein pulsed angrily in his forehead. Jerry's face went ghostly grey as he strained to read those lips and absorbed his father's frustration.

When the lecture ended, Jerry turned back to me and sighed, as if he could exhale his embarrassment in a single breath. I followed the arc of his long fingers as he gestured back toward the Heights High athletic fields. He smiled, rambling on about 1950 and I knew he was blocking out his life today, his wife and twelve-year-old daughter gone, somewhere in Illinois.

My mother said that Aunt Terri was mentally ill, and that she and Sue were wandering around Chicago. Meanwhile, Jerry remained in Cleveland, working as a draftsman's assistant and crafting blueprints for the architects who'd supervised him for the past seven years. On his drafting table, the world was reduced to schematic drawings and clean angled lines, pictures my uncle could decode, shapes that made sense.

Jerry had been educated orally; his teachers told him he must "overcome his handicap," must speak, read lips and strain to understand those who could hear, and he tried, desperately. Instead of sending Jerry to the Ohio School for the Deaf in faraway Columbus, my grandparents enrolled him in a special oral program for deaf children in the nearby suburb of East Cleveland. There sign language was strictly forbidden. Jerry was separated from the deaf world; I'd never seen my uncle sign, and wasn't sure if he knew how. Jerry's teachers had taught him that "sign" wasn't a language at all, just a series of crude animal-like gestures, unfit for human consumption. So Jerry existed in a world of pantomime, lipreading and broken speech, a world he inhabited alone.

As a young boy, my uncle learned to speak in jarring tones, his accents often on the wrong syllables, his pronunciation harsh and edgy. Still, talking at all was quite a feat for a profoundly deaf boy who had never heard the sound of a human voice. He graduated from Cleveland Heights High School, the first deaf student to do so, (several others followed), and earned his varsity letters.

It seemed to me that Jerry never found his place in the adult world, where most of his classmates went on to college and the professions. My grandparents didn't consider higher education a realistic choice for Jerry, who struggled in subjects like history and reading and didn't seem interested in school. Papa Ben pushed Jerry to learn a trade instead. Eventually, Papa helped Jerry get a job with a local architect, who trained my uncle to make architectural drawings. Jerry held his job at the firm for many years, until his death.

By the time I was paying attention, Jerry was a 40-year-old ex-jock with the hint of a paunch, though he still carried himself with a long-limbed grace, an athlete's confidence when playing ball or dancing, where his body knew what to do, when speech and hearing were not required.

•

During high school, Jerry stood above his hearing classmates, both literally and figuratively. He was two or three years older and ultimately taller than most of them, though he didn't grow to his full 6'3" until he was 17. He was called "Jinx" in the neighborhood, though no one was sure how he'd earned the nickname. Maybe it was mockery at first, the misfortune of being different in an era when disability was a source of shame.

But by his sophomore and junior years in high school, Jinx Cohen was a handsome, well-liked athlete. If he didn't really understand what most of his teachers were saying—a skilled lip-reader, he didn't possess X-ray vision, couldn't see through the back of their heads as they wrote on the chalkboard, or peer beneath a teacher's mustache—he was fluent in the social whirl of Cleveland Heights High and the sports that presented one road to popularity. The visual dance of the basketball court, the rushing breeze of the high hurdles, the pulsing bass of the dance floor—those he knew well. His physical style, combined with a ready smile and good looks, were enough to get by.

Jerry graduated in 1951, unsure of what would come next. He lost touch with his old friends, some of whom, like his cousin Bobby, had already gone off to the military, or on to college. They got married and started their families and careers. For several years, Jerry remained at home with Nanny and Papa, working odd jobs, still tethered to his parents. He visited the Deaf Club in Akron, learned some basic sign language, and played basketball on a deaf team. He went to deaf tournaments and danced during the inevitable parties organized by the host clubs, the music blasting through the walls and floor, the way deaf people like it.

Even at the deaf club, Jerry restrained himself, gesturing, using his speech and signing only when he got excited, particularly when he talked about sports. When he signed it was choppy, awkward, marking him as an "oral deaf" man who regarded sign language as an embarrassment.

My uncle reminded me of the golden boys I idolized during my own high school years, the athletes who swaggered down the brick hallways of Beachwood High, their black and gold lettermen's jackets reflecting their place in the school community. Twenty years later, Jerry was still pining for that world, and there was something sad about that.

All my grandparents' efforts to help Jerry "assimilate"—the speech therapy, the tutors, the denial of sign language and the focus on spoken English—could only take him so far. Once high school was over, there was no clear pathway—neither higher education nor the industries such as printing, into which many deaf people were channeled—for Jerry to pursue.

Now he lived on the margins, caught between memories of his 'hearing' high school and the years that came after, years that would bring more than his share of disappointment. Papa Ben never lost his palpable sense of frustration around Jerry. Now, looking back, I know that Papa saw Jerry—his only son—as a pale reflection of himself, as a damaged man who would never be able to take over the family business.

Like Jerry, I too was different: painfully thin at 15, still waiting for puberty years after my friends had arrived. Afraid of gym class and team sports, of showing my lack of manhood in the locker room, and of getting into fights, I simply wanted to survive high school, to get my diploma and get out. One boy, a thick, pudgy kid who outweighed me by 40 pounds, bullied me for many years. Several times we fought, briefly, until Howie sat on my face and I gave in.

Unlike Jerry, I could almost pass for normal, despite my shyness and puny awkward body. But I felt a connection with him, for reasons I couldn't identify as a child. Neither Jerry nor I had the language to discuss our sense of difference. Attracted to boys, and sometimes to men, I was cut off from others by this thing I couldn't reveal to anyone.

Sometimes, on weekend nights when I was a teenager, I stayed over at Nanny and Papa's house, and Jerry and I would watch wrestling. Entranced by the moving images, my uncle smiled and cheered; it was a dance he knew well, no captions needed. I enjoyed the show too, but for different reasons, for the excitement that wended through me, forbidden, mixed with guilt and shame about the objects of my attraction.

Uncle Jerry leaned toward the black-and-white TV, sitting on the edge of his twin bed, eyes fixed on the screen, the action reflected in his dark pupils. I squirmed on the other bed, keeping my shirt un-tucked, disguising my arousal. Raymond Rougeau and Luis Martinez squared off, a handsome young Canadian and a savvy Mexican. Rougeau wore blue briefs that showed off his muscular butt, Martinez black ones that emphasized his toughness and experience. Jerry pointed to Martinez and nodded. "He's gonna kill that boy." I rooted for the underdog—Rougeau—as he took a shot to the midsection and fell at the feet of the Mexican. Transfixed by the struggle, I memorized the muscular curves of Rougeau's thighs, the ample mounds of his pecs. Jerry enjoyed the contest too, pretending it was real, forgetting that it wasn't.

•

One Sunday afternoon about a year later, when I was 16, I went over to my grandparents' house after a session of Dale Carnegie's "How to Win Friends and Influence People" course, which was sponsored by the Cleveland chapter of Junior Achievement. "JA" was a non-profit organization designed to teach high-school students good citizenship and respect for business, a decidedly uncool activity in the early 1970s. Still, it provided me with a means to meet teens from the surrounding suburbs, and of making friends beyond the narrow Jewish world of my hometown.

The course met on eight consecutive Sundays, and required us to read several of the late Carnegie's books. Those books seemed simplistic, outdated, and manipulative to me even then, as a high school sophomore. Still, I figured exposure to Carnegie's loopy optimism couldn't hurt given my inbred pessimism, and I liked giving a weekly speech on given topics like, "The Best Vacation I Ever Had," "The Person I Admire the Most," and "How I Overcame my Fear of ___." Though my speeches have faded from memory, I did win two special pens, one for "Most Improved" and one for "Best Speech of the Day," which allowed me a few fleeting moments of pride.

On that particular Sunday, I walked into Nanny and Papa's ranch home with its crown insignia on the garage door, as if they—Cohens and Weinbaums—were descended from royalty instead of Russian-Jewish peasants. I came upon Uncle Jerry sitting on the gold-cushioned sofa in my grandparents' den, his arm draped around the shoulders of a dark-haired doe-eyed woman, his fingers resting on her shoulder. She beamed at him, black eyebrows arched over heavy-lashed brown eyes, which gave her a startled expression.

I was startled, too; this woman bore an uncanny resemblance to Jerry's first wife, my Aunt Terri. But she could hear, had normal speech, and introduced herself as Renee. As Renee shook my hand, Jerry smiled, his brown eyes watching her as she explained, through painted lips, how they'd met at a singles' dance.

Renee and Jerry were both divorced, around 40, and loved to dance. Overnight, it seemed, Jerry had acquired a fiancée. A few months later they were married, in a low-key ceremony that seemed to reflect my grandparents' low expectations for the match and the reality of a second marriage.

My recollections of the wedding have merged with a series of photographs taken in a small chapel at Heights Temple. I recall the wedding party—my uncle, tall and almost bald, his oval head and broad generous ears standing out, looking like an older, looser version of the man I'd known my whole life. Renee, two heads shorter, stood next to Jerry in a poufy, off-white dress. My grandparents were nearby, Papa decked out in an old sport-coat, his mustache neatly trimmed, Nanny beside him with her lacquered-blonde bouffant curls, over-sized white plastic-framed glasses and checkered dress, both looking pleased and possibly relieved that Jerry was moving out. My parents, my brother Alex and I stood off to one side, smiling for posterity.

Renee's children were there, too. Her son Ronnie, a year younger than I, was already more savvy in the ways of the world and seemed vaguely dangerous with his olive skin, long black hair, dark eyes, and permanent smirk. In his wide-lapelled jacket and black dress shirt, Ronnie was both handsome and edgy. I'd heard whispers that he'd been "in trouble" with drugs in high school. A decade before he'd have been called a juvenile delinquent. His younger sister, Melissa, was troubled, too. Melissa reminded me of Tatum O'Neal, a plump, whiny girl of 10 or 11, prone to tantrums. A few years later, she'd be sent off to a residential school for emotionally disturbed children.

My uncle's marriage would be rocky. At first, my mother reported that he and Renee seemed happy. Some months into the marriage, I heard there were "problems," centered on Renee's difficult children. By that time, I rarely saw Jerry and gave little thought to his struggles; I was consumed with my own: I had defended my virginal girlfriend's honor when one of the jocks on the golf team snickered that she was "trash," as we passed him on the way to class. That led to a brief fight in the high school cafeteria, where I landed a punch to his shoulder before he rocked my head. I got off easily, but was not anxious for round two. Underneath my need to defend my girlfriend—who hadn't even heard the insult and laughed the whole thing off—was my need to stand up for myself, to make up for all those times I had run away from fat Howard, my neighborhood tormentor, and beneath that, my call to deny those desires I couldn't name, and to prove I was normal.

14

A year after the wedding, in the fall of 1974, I was circulating at Alex's Bar-Mitzvah party at the Host House Party Center, east of Cleveland. I played the role of older brother, mingling with the crowd, collecting hugs and congratulations on my good grades and newfound height. Papa Ben and Nanny Fay, assorted cousins from Columbus and Steubenville, and my parents' friends had shown up for the occasion. After growing half a foot in the past year, I was taller than most of the men—but not Uncle Jerry. To my right, I saw him and Renee head for the band.

On this night, gliding to the dance floor, leading his second wife by the hand, my uncle was radiant. Smiling, teeth visible, Jerry's forehead glistened under the chandeliered lights as he led Renee toward a gap on the wooden floor. Loose-limbed and relaxed, his black shoes shined to a high sheen, he swiveled toward his wife and began to move to the beat, which pulsated through his body, rocking from the inside out. Renee turned toward him, moving up and back, shimmying in her slinky black skirt. She laughed, open-mouthed, eyes framed by her black eyeliner and teased hair. Soon their hips were rocking side to side as she spun out to the beat. Jerry tapped his long, narrow feet, fingers snapping in time with the music. The band's singer launched into Aretha Franklin's "R-E-S-P-E-C-T/take care—TCB," and my uncle was with her, getting down, rocking out. No one could tell him that he was not whole, not full, not right for this one night…

•

Several months later, I met an old high school classmate of my mother's on a family trip to Israel. She, as it happened, was the director of a program for deaf children in Lakewood, a suburb on Cleveland's West Side. I told her I hoped to become a teacher and was curious to see classes for the deaf. A few weeks later, I visited the school.

There, for the very first time, I saw deaf children signing, fingers flying, gesturing in an easy natural way I'd never seen from Jerry. In fact, years later I learned that my uncle had forbidden Aunt Terri and Sue from using sign language at home. Terri had gone to the Central Institute for the Deaf in St. Louis and was educated in the oral method, like Jerry. But Terri picked up sign language in the school dorms and signed whenever she could. Despite Jerry's complaints, Terri taught Sue to sign before she could talk, and used it with her each morning after my uncle went to work. I never saw Jerry sign, just heard him talk in his flat deaf speech, his vowels elongated as if English were a foreign tongue.

Watching those children sign, I felt a visceral excitement and knew in that moment I had found my calling. I'm not sure if I mentioned my visit to the school or my future plans to Jerry when I saw him on Passover, our annual spring ritual at Nanny and Papa's. But I didn't connect my choice to become a teacher with my uncle's deafness. It was simply a fascination with sign language and my instinctive attraction to people on the margins that drew me in.

•

One humid evening in early May, about a month after Passover, I came in through the back door of my parents' house. A blast of cool air met me in the hallway, along with Alex.

"It's Uncle Jerry—he had a heart attack and was rushed to Hillcrest Hospital. He's dead," my brother said. I felt numb, suspended, my ears buzzing as if my hearing were fading. This can't be happening, not to my only uncle who is 44 years old, and who in the last few months had seemed happy, like he was at my brother's bar-mitzvah.

But of course it had happened, and there was more to come.

Chapter 3

What Remained

On a stifling July day a few weeks after my high school graduation, I walked in our back door, surrounded by the silver kitchen wallpaper that reminded me of gift-wrap. There I saw my mother's scribbled note on the white Formica counter—"Papa collapsed at store rushed to St. Alexis—Hurry!"—and I did, running out to the old Chevy Bel-Air that was parked out back. The rusted out Chevy had become mine the year before, when my parents bought my grandfather a new car, another blue Chevrolet.

St. Alexis Hospital was located near East 55th Street, down in the old neighborhood by Papa's store. I didn't know the exact location of the hospital but headed southwest, retracing my grandfather's daily route along Harvard Avenue, the one he'd driven a thousand times in this same Chevy.

My grandfather wasn't physically imposing. In a picture on our family room wall there was Papa on his wedding day, complete with long suit jacket and cutaway tails, a pencil mustache, and a boutonniere. The man I knew still had the same hint of mischief in his hooded eyes, the same beaklike nose and thin mustache, now flecked with gray. But his body was worn down, his clothes dusted with ash and marked with cigarette burns, a testament to his love for smoke and the ever-present Camels that gave his voice its raspy quality, a mix of warmth and harsh.

Despite Papa's general air of fatigue, pride and self-satisfaction radiated from him; he knew his place in the world. He walked through it chest out, a bantamweight ready for whatever life could throw him. And life had thrown a lot, though I didn't know the details back then. He'd grown up poor with his immigrant parents, the oldest child and son. A bright boy with a curious mind, he raced through high school, graduating at 16, and went on to pharmacy school at Ohio State, settling for a shorter path than the one he really wanted—that led to medical school, to become a doctor. He met my grandmother, a few years older, on the train to Columbus. He was cocky, charming, a young flaneur with a mustache like Adolphe Menjou, and how could she not fall for him, which is exactly what she did.

Fay was going to visit her brother Frank, who was in dental school at OSU. In the freewheeling '20s, she was a young woman with a good job—office manager at the White Sewing Machine Company—and on the side she modeled furs for I. J. Fox, her fur-covered form gracing ads in the Cleveland papers. Soon they were dating, and then engaged. Ben seemed like a good catch; though poor, he'd become a licensed pharmacist at the tender age of 19, though he'd needed special permission from the governor to do so.

Then the losses began to pile up—Jerry's deafness, Fay's Bell's palsy, her crying jags and "nervous condition," for which my grandfather never got a good diagnosis. How much of her depression was caused by her guilt in producing a handicapped child, a son who couldn't hear her silky voice or Ben's raspy one? Soon after Jerry was born, my grandmother lost much of her own hearing. The doctors called it "calcification," bone growth in the middle ear. A strange coincidence, a twist of fate, that her son would be born deaf, his auditory nerves dead, and then her own hearing faded. There was talk of German measles or rubella during her pregnancy, as well as a fall during her 7th month, as possible causes of Jerry's deafness. Regardless, he would never hear his mother's voice.

If Papa could not cure his deaf son, he was determined to help his hard of hearing wife. He took my grandmother to specialists near and far. One surgeon performed a fenestration, removing extra bone from Fay's ears, but it quickly grew back, like her guilt.

Through it all Papa kept working, until he became the man I knew; if not content, then resigned to the various frustrations of family, adjustments that must be made. Still, he had his daughter and her marriage to a good provider, and their three sons to go along with Jerry's little girl, who was born, thankfully, with normal hearing.

He had the store, too, a testament to a half-century of day-in and day-out work, his hard won respect in the neighborhood, the business that put his daughter through three years of college, which should have been four, if only she hadn't dropped out to marry Bill, and why couldn't she have waited a year? And Papa had Jerry who would always be needing help, but at least he was working, had a stable job if not a good first marriage and it was too bad his first wife was not just deaf, but crazy, and now Jerry had issues with his second wife who was just as crazy as the first and his son could sure pick 'em, but what could he do beyond giving Jerry advice he didn't want to hear?

Through it all Papa ministered to Slavic Village, gave his customers their medicine with bits of advice he dispensed for free. In his store, he was secure among glass jars, metal scales, dusty shelves. This was life in balance as it rarely was within the confines of his family. My mother, his oldest, the one who should have earned the college degree that Jerry could not, urged him to cut back, sell the store, retire. The idea held no allure for him.

And do what?

His life was pressed into those shelves, the sweat-stained wood, the cluttered counters and magazine racks at the corner of East 71st and Harvard Avenue. In the gray light of Harvard Drug, Papa could be the healer he'd imagined himself to be fifty years earlier, the aspiring doctor who earned his pharmacy degree in three years and put his brother Itz through school, too, who took care of his parents and his sister Lil until she was married off to a young accountant.

19

The store supported Fay, Rita and Jerry, along with Itz and his brother's young family. It took care of Fay's doctors and Jerry's endless rounds of speech therapy, of all the services the boy needed just to speak so that people could—sometimes, but not always— understand him. The store provided Papa with a good living, so he couldn't complain and rarely did.

•

Even now, long after I'd taken possession, the car still smelled of my grandfather and his Camel filters, burning ash held between tapered fingers. He would set them down, forgotten, where they bored into the Chevy's blue dashboard and gray cloth seats, pock-marked like a teenager with acne. Papa smoked constantly, absent-mindedly. Half-smoked cigarettes lay around him at the store, turning the air sour, blue smoke tracing curvy lines through the air, his nimble fingers stained yellow from nicotine.

A layer of gray film coated the windshield and windows. Still the car ran, stubbornly resisting my grandfather's and then my own inadvertent attempts to break it down.

I sped west down Harvard as it bisected the city, from Green Road in the eastern suburbs into the city of Cleveland itself, my stomach tensed. Heading toward the old Polish neighborhood where the store was located, the houses grew closer together, in formation, two-family homes with sagging front porches and splin-tered paint.

As I passed John F. Kennedy High School the neighborhood was suddenly all black. Eventually I passed into the ethnic enclave that had, after several decades, woven my grandfather into its heart while holding out against integration, against outsiders. Still, its days as a center of Polish life were numbered, the sons and daugh-ters flowing out to suburban Parma on the west side and Garfield Heights on the east.

I reached 55th Street and Broadway, the commercial center of the neighborhood, and found my way to the hospital. It wasn't far. I must have asked for directions, but I remember only running through the parking lot, heart pumping, and entering the dark coolness of the building. Even then, it seemed ironic—my grandfather Cohen, a proud if unobservant Jew—in this most Catholic of hospitals. Stepping out of an elevator I saw, on a cushioned bench, my mother and grandmother huddled together beneath a gold cross. I knew I was too late.

A few minutes later a black orderly wheeled a gurney, body covered by a white sheet past us and into the elevator. My mother's prediction, one she'd murmur like an incantation throughout my childhood after pleading with Papa to finally retire, "Your grandfather's gonna die at that store," proved true.

•

Over the next several weeks, I worked in the dank confines of Papa's store without him, though the counters, walls, and floors were infused with his being. Those plank floors, remnants from the 1920s, when Papa had purchased Harvard Drug from another druggist, creaked under my feet. How many times had he paced those same floorboards, searched the rows of dark shelves stuffed with toiletries and medicines in a system known only to him, looking for one particular remedy?

In my memory the store is brown and gray, dust motes circling in the filtered light, which streamed in along with dirt and noise from the intersection of East 71st Street and Harvard Avenue. The store sat too close to that busy interchange—one driver in the early 1970s destroyed the plate glass storefront when he lost control of his car. During those oppressive days of summer the front door was propped open, a ceiling fan stirring the thick, coal-dusted air, which floated up from the nearby steel mills that hummed along the Cuyahoga River.

I stood behind the front counter, selling cigarettes and candy bars as I had on occasional Saturdays as a boy, when I'd accompany Papa to the store. Once there, I'd stock and re-stock his magazines, sell Necco wafers, Chesterfield cigarettes and Polish newspapers to the men and women who trickled into the pharmacy. By 3 or 4 o'clock, Papa would close up and we'd head out to Cleveland Heights to a greasy luncheonette called Mawby's, famous for its mouth-watering grilled hamburgers topped with onions, their scent making me salivate like one of Pavlov's dogs.

Now I worked behind that same counter, trying not to think of Papa laid out on this same wooden floor after falling off a ladder due to something called an "aortic aneurysm." Now, making change out of the register drawer, the crank of the gilded cash register broken years before. The smells of the store and the surrounding neighborhood—diesel fuel, soot, and ash—mixed with my sweat while when my parents brought in a rotating cast of pharmacists to fill prescriptions, to keep the store going, to find a buyer.

What remained in the weeks after my uncle's and grandfather's deaths were magazines that would never be read, beauty powder that would never be sold, and the old phone booth with the 1930's-style Ohio Bell Telephone symbol embossed in gold leaf, which sat silent, empty. What remained were the old folks, neighborhood women in worn print dresses and babushkas and men in sweat-stained collared shirts, who came in to pay their respects to Uncle Itz, Papa's long-time partner, now partially crippled by a stroke. He could no longer fill prescriptions but sat at a small table in the front of the store, sipping coffee and weeping silently.

There were no buyers for Papa's little business. Instead, my parents sold his customer list to another pharmacist, a younger Jew with a store in the neighborhood, for $2,000. Then they hired an auctioneer, a grizzled hillbilly with white hair and a matching beard to strip the store clean. Working under his direction, Alex and I salvaged anything we could, from the rusted out 'Drink Coca-Cola' sign, which was anchored into the brick on the Harvard Avenue side of the building, to bottles and bottles of unsold medicine. The sign, a burnt-red bottle cap perched above the store's entrance, groaned as I leaned out a second-story window and strained to dislodge it. Eventually, with an assist from the lean but powerful auctioneer, the cap popped free and clattered to the sidewalk below. It was hard, in that moment, not to think of my grandfather.

The auctioneer, focused on his task, loaded everything into a large truck. Back outside his store we emptied those liquid medicines into a plastic bucket, creating a toxic blend that made me nauseous. A mound of colored glass, purple, red and sea green, lay alongside the bucket, the remnants of potions for customers long dead and gone. Over time, I came to see Papa's death, so soon after Jerry's as a rupture of the heart, a final loss my grandfather could not contain.

Chapter 4

Crossing Over

September 5, 1962. My first day of school is embedded in my memory, a bug trapped in amber.

My mother, who had just earned her driver's license, carefully piloted our orange Mercury Comet station wagon over the half-mile distance from our house to Canterbury School. As we approached the immensity of the playground and ball-fields, her lacquered nails tapped the steering wheel. I'd been invited, along with the other boys and girls in my kindergarten class, for a 'meet and greet' session, the day before classes were to begin.

We filed in quietly, scoping out our new classroom while clutching the hands of our mothers. Under the hum of fluorescent lights, the sights of the school absorbed me—the green linoleum floor, the beige window shades, and the commanding presence of my new teacher, Mrs. Ullner, a prune-faced woman with stiff gray-black hair and oversized cat's eye glasses. A warm breeze blew through the open windows, adding the scent of freshly cut grass to the institutional aroma of ammonia mixed with Comet.

"By the end of September, you will know these by heart." Gesturing with a wooden pointer, her posture stiff as her hair, Mrs. Ullner read her classroom rules out loud. The rules, which none of us could read, included reminders like, "Do not run in the classroom," "Raise your hands and not your voice," and "Act like young ladies and gentlemen." Sitting on the brown oval-shaped rug in one corner of the small classroom, I felt my stomach churn and rumble. How could I spend a whole day with this old woman?

Knowing I had no choice, I kept my doubts to myself. After the meeting ended, we rode over to Scott's Five and Dime, where my mother bought me a bottle of blow-bubbles, a box of Jujy-Fruits, and a yellow plastic whistle.

When we got back home, my mother described the plan she'd devised to get me safely to and from school. We lived at 3665 Silsby Road, on a busy two-lane street I'd have to cross on a daily basis. Each morning, Mom would guide me to the other side, and then go back home to take care of my brother Alex, who was barely a year old, while I walked on alone. (My older brother Doug, who also attended Canterbury, was a 5th grader with no interest in escorting me to school. If my parents had asked, he would have flat out refused). In the afternoons, I'd reach the far side of Silsby, toot my whistle, and once again, my mother would usher me to safety.

I stood on the sidewalk across the rutted street from home, my heart pounding. Mom, in a red vinyl jacket, entered our house, closed the creaky front door and disappeared behind its diamond-shaped windows. I squeezed the whistle, felt its plastic weightlessness, its impotence and silence. Looking around for another adult, I spotted a gardener mowing the lawn behind me; I heard the thrum of his lawnmower, smelled its gasoline. He was someone I could ask for help—the thought passed through my mind—but I quickly dismissed it; as a big boy, I should do this alone.

My mother lay across a chasm. It widened as I waited, ten beats or twenty, an eternity. Then, launched by adrenaline, I bolted into the street, stretching for the other side. A green Pontiac, complete with fins, swooshed by and then I was flying spinning sinking, dropping onto asphalt, my left hip shattered and my mind numb.

•

I woke in a crib-like hospital bed, my left leg hung skyward at a 45-degree angle, in traction to prevent movement. Even my head was locked in place—I'd sustained a concussion, too. But my head healed quickly, and soon I could sit halfway up and examine the hospital ward where I was marooned. The children's ward of Suburban Hospital was a long, narrow room with two rows of beds on opposite walls, the residents facing each other. Encased in whiteness, surrounded by white walls and sheets, I didn't find much to capture my attention—other than the boy who slept in the bed next to mine.

The boy, named Roger, had been diagnosed with "walking pneumonia," but he could do anything he wanted--short of going home. Since I couldn't move around, I exercised my imagination, with Roger as my muse. Besides watching Sherri Lewis and Lambchop, and Kukla, Fran and Ollie, we invented a game called "Tarzan Treehouse." Inspired by the movies that popped up on the television that sat on a ledge above our beds, the game involved scary adventures in which Roger played Tarzan and I became Jane. Over the past year, I'd developed a strange fascination with that beefy man in a loincloth, and felt a rising excitement whenever he swung onto the screen.

During our games, I wove stories of adventure, inspiring Roger to save me from evil white hunters—usually Germans—who attacked our jungle home or abducted Cheetah. Cooking and cleaning like Mom did for Dad, I sautéed elephant and stewed rhinoceros, and served up meals with a flourish. But Roger, unlike my father, never complained that our dinners weren't to his liking.

After a few weeks, the ward began to empty. Kids with tonsillitis, rubella and chicken pox went home, until only Roger and I remained. Soon I learned that my friend was going home, too, leaving me alone with my Tarzan movies. Roger's parents—his father decked out in a brown wool suit, his mother dolled up like Donna Reed in a shiny dress and matching shoes, were packing Roger's things while his doctor "took a last listen" to my roommate's bony chest. "Hmmm," the doctor said; there was a rattle, a slight wheeze. I almost shouted with relief; my friend would be with me until the end.

The days ran together, time marked by my father's visits after work, the feel of his big hands tousling my hair, his gifts of Lance butter cookies and tart Pez candies in their clown dispensers from the hospital gift shop. Mom came by each afternoon, her face creased with worry, and Roger and I played our games and spun our stories. Finally, in early October, I went into surgery, was released from traction, and put into a long plaster cast, which covered my left leg like a sleeve.

A few days later, it was my turn to go home. Roger walked near my wheelchair as Dad steered me toward the parking lot. Picking me up like a particularly valuable sack of groceries, my father stowed me in the back of our station wagon. Roger stood in the doorway, waving. My throat closed as we pulled away, and I waved back to my shrinking friend until he was no longer visible. I would never see him again.

Propped up in the living room, so I wouldn't have to tackle the stairs, I surveyed our pale beech furniture, the aqua blue ottoman and pink sectional sofa. Dust spiraled over the gray light of our television. The TV became my babysitter as Mom looked after Doug and Alex, who was just beginning to walk and talk, while my father worked six days a week, establishing his electrical contracting business. At his office just east of downtown, Dad pored over blueprints, made bids, and fought for the right to put electrical wiring into the big steel mills along the Cuyahoga River.

Eventually, I freed myself from my hospital bed and scooted around the floors of our house, watched over by my mother and our latest cleaning lady. A few days before Halloween, a surgeon finally removed my cast. Cutting the white casing in two, the doctor exposed my yellow-white left leg for the first time in seven weeks. I gasped. The withered left leg had shrunk to half the width of my right.

At first, I could not walk. My leg ached, and my muscles couldn't support my weight. But on the night before Halloween, determined to get my share of candy, I pushed myself up against our pink sofa and stumbled onto my feet. Lurching around the living room like a kindergartner who'd drunk too much Passover wine, I called out to show my parents. The next night Dad guided me out the door, as I carefully climbed my neighbors' stoops, a miniature reflection of Zorro. I greedily collected Clark bars, Chunkies, and Necco wafers, allowing my father to carry me to the last few houses, when my rubbery leg wouldn't support me.

No one welcomed me back into the world of kindergarten. Mrs. Ullner seemed unconcerned about the accident, and annoyed by my presence in her classroom. By December, I walked to school alone--panting, sweating, and crying. I had no nightmares, only a constant terror that propelled me faster during every trip to and from school, a fear that I wouldn't find my way home, and that I'd be lost forever.

•

One morning in March, I raced toward school, breathless, the scent of wet grass, mud and daffodils enveloping me. Mrs. Ullner chatted with another teacher as I ran into the antiseptic space of our classroom, safe at last. Blinking from behind her glasses, she frowned, regarding me with skepticism.

"Here's that crybaby—the one I was telling you about," she said, gesturing in my direction. "None of the other boys or girls cry. What's wrong with you?"

I said nothing; it was hard enough just to breathe. I ate her words like sand. I had been weighed, judged, found wanting. My teacher had confirmed my fears—I was truly different from everyone else. The whole thing was my fault.

It was 1962, and five-year-old boys walked to school alone, did not cry, and did not dream of a boy named Roger.

•

28

Many years later, I discovered that a car had hit Jerry, too. According to his cousin Bobby, who lived down the street and went to school with my uncle, a group of boys were hanging out in front of Bobby's house on Cummings Road, one spring day during the war years. A few of the boys were teasing the 12-year-old Jerry—making fun of his atonal deaf speech—and one pulled a pea-shooter out of the pocket of his dungarees, hitting him in the neck. Jerry stepped back into the street, moving out of range, when a car came careening around the corner onto Cummings, a car that Jerry did not see and could not hear. Before the boys could react, Jerry was spread out before them, still conscious and howling, his leg battered and bleeding. An ambulance transported him and his mother Fay down to Mt. Sinai Hospital in the city, where he was bandaged up and eventually sent home. The wound healed, leaving few if any physical scars, only emotional ones that would erupt in the years to come.

Chapter 5

The Supplicant

Papa Ben faced an architect half his age, a 30-year-old still wet behind the ears, across the expanse of the young man's desktop. Papa, wearing an old sports-coat in muted brown wool, held his fedora, fingered the brim. Brian, the architect, would have been comfortable, composed, at home, sitting in his office on a sunny spring day in 1965. A young man on the rise—his parents would be proud, my grandfather might have thought.

Maybe Papa knew them. There were few degrees of separation among Cleveland's East Side Jews, a bustling community of 80,000 souls. At 60, Bernard Cohen, (everyone called him Ben), looked worn and disheveled. He'd long ago surrendered the stylish young man in his wedding photo, weighed down by work and family ties. Papa's picture was paired with one of Nanny Fay, a petite, striking woman in a layered wedding dress, whose delicate beauty bore little resemblance to the sickly, hard-of-hearing woman I knew as my grandmother.

In the photograph, Papa sits on a bench, his lean body turned to one side, face angled back toward the photographer. Wearing a tuxedo jacket with boutonniere, his eyes are at half-mast, his face radiating a relaxed pleasure—the cat who'd just imbibed a can of tuna.

Now, Ben Cohen was simply tired. His often-ill wife who was no longer beautiful, his son would never hear, there were long hours at the store—early morning till night—and yet, most of the time, he seemed content, with a touch of resignation. His workdays at Harvard Drug near the steel mills down on the Southeast Side, and his dinners at home, Jewish rye, chicken soup and pickled herring with my grandmother, (an excellent cook but a bird-like eater), gave Papa's days a regular rhythm; he became a creature of habit, a human metronome. Despite the disorder in his car and the jumbled recesses of the store, Papa doted on his customers, his place in the world secure.

But Jerry's situation weighed on my grandfather. After high school, Jerry had tried printing—a common occupation for deaf people in the 1950s, since they were impervious to the noise of the presses—but found it boring and repetitive. Jobs were hard to find, and Jerry had never learned to read well.

Eventually he took a job at Lake Erie Electric, my father's electrical contracting business. Dad's work as an electrical engineer was far beyond Jerry's knowledge and training; he was marking time, sketching blueprints until something better came along. Jerry's position at my father's firm was a favor repaid—Papa had given my parents the money for a down payment on their first home. And my father respected my grandfather, for his integrity and Jewish work ethic, his determination to succeed at the drug store.

By 1965, Jerry was 35, with a wife and daughter. Papa wanted security and a regular paycheck for his only son, beyond what my father could give him; I assume Jerry wanted something similar.

Ben Cohen didn't like asking for favors. Rather he was used to granting them in the hazy confines of his store. For 40 years, ever since he'd taken over Harvard Drug in the mid-1920s, Papa had been helping out the factory-workers and their hard-working wives, the bedrock of the neighborhood.

The store sat in a close-knit neighborhood just this side of poor. Papa wouldn't refuse a mother, a husband, a son their needed medicine. They'd pay if and when they could. Most did, eventually. In the meantime, they knew where to find my grandfather, sleeves rolled up, bifocals perched on his long nose, mixing medicines six or seven days a week, a Camel cigarette placed nearby, burning to ash. Ben Cohen had literally fought his way into Slavic Village; now, after four decades, he embodied it—a living, breathing symbol of the cracked sidewalks, potholed streets and listing double-deckers along East 71st Street.

Papa sat across from Brian, the young architect, a supplicant, a plea reflected in his dark eyes. He lit up a Camel, exhaled smoke through his nostrils and smiled. It turned out that one of Papa's friend's sons was the architect's best buddy from high school, part of the tribal web that wove Jews together. And Brian had known Jerry, superficially, when they were both teenagers. Brian was two years younger than Jerry and had gone to Glenville High School down in Cleveland, several miles from Cleveland Heights. But they'd played pick-up basketball together at Cain Park, where Jerry stood out more for his speed and athletic prowess than his inability to hear.

Papa told Brian about Jerry's interest in drawing, his manual dexterity, and his willingness to work. Would he be willing to take Jerry on?

The young architect agreed, and suddenly my uncle had a new job. Papa reached across Brian's mahogany desk and shook the man's hand, smiling under his wispy mustache. Papa said, "Deaf people are very insecure about what's going on around them. If Jerry looks up and sees people at one end of a room and they're clustered together, he'll think they're talking about him."

And so Brian learned that my uncle's natural responses were essentially paranoid, Papa's belief reflecting the common thinking of the time.

Over the next decade, Jerry worked for Brian as the firm grew. Meanwhile, my grandfather kept on working at the store, six days a week if not seven, ignoring my mother's entreaties to retire or, "Take a vacation for God's sake." At least Papa didn't have to worry about Jerry's employment; from then on he had a steady paycheck.

At first, my uncle was a "jack of all trades" at the firm, picking up packages, running errands and overseeing the print room where all the blueprints were copied. Later, one of the architects tried to train Jerry to become a draftsman, giving him technical manuals to study. But Jerry couldn't fully comprehend those manuals, which explained the mechanics of drafting. Other draftsmen were hired, surpassing him, creating blueprints from scratch, while my uncle served as a draftsman's assistant, his blueprints marked up, specs written in. Then Jerry would create new drawings, following the visual directions of the architects, which he could decipher.

Though Jerry wasn't distracted by sound, his concentration was erratic, like his ability to read. Perhaps he dreamed of being an architect himself, or an artist. No one, including Brian, seemed to know.

Still, Brian was fond of Jerry; he described him as "colorful and unique" in our conversation more than 30 years after Jerry's death. But trying to get specifics, searching for scraps of the uncle I never fully knew, I heard what I'd heard before—he was an athlete. He was social, and would dance with anyone at the firm's office parties.

He was also anxious, frustrated and angry. Sometimes Jerry would yell at a co-worker, or mumble out loud to himself, suppressed rage bubbling to the surface. Still, according to Brian, it never got out of hand at the office. But, (I learned much later) his rage often spilled over when he got home to the apartment he shared with his first wife and their only child.

Today I wonder how Jerry felt about being the only deaf man in a hearing office, an anomaly, almost a mascot. When I suggested, three decades later, that Jerry didn't fit in either the Deaf or hearing worlds, Brian said, "That explains the intensity," and I knew, in that moment, that he had a sense of Jerry in his later years that few people, deaf or hearing, ever did. And still, there was much he didn't know—of Jerry's capacity for violence, of the rage that went beyond "agitation," of his profound isolation.

Jerry liked to tell stories, too, and shared some of them with his boss. Jerry's voice would rise and pick up speed, sailing off into the upper registers, and "I'd get the point of the story, even if I couldn't understand all of it," Brian told me years later.

Another piece of the puzzle clicked into place. How many conversations did I have with my only uncle between the ages of four and eighteen? No more than a few dozen. But I don't recall struggling to understand him. Now it was clear that other people—hearing people without deaf relatives—did—even those who saw him daily.

I asked Brian, finally, if he could refer me to others who knew Jerry during his years at the firm. He couldn't; my uncle didn't socialize with co-workers outside of the office. Still, today the firm does a lot of design work for the handicapped. That, according to Brian, is Jerry's legacy.

As the conversation wound down, Brian told me once again how much he liked Jerry, and frequently remembered him. Later, I listened to the interview once again, turning the architect's spare memories over in my mind, examining each shard and fragment. I have so little of my uncle.

Chapter 6

Passing Over

We sat around a long table and read responsively from our Maxwell House haggadahs. The story of the Jews' deliverance from Egypt went back thousands of years to the time of Moses, a far cry from the daily concerns of a nine-year-old boy in 1966. Still, I loved the special foods, the proscribed rituals, and the four questions of the Passover seder, each based on the first one: 'Why is this night different from all other nights?'

Though my parents and grandparents were not "observant," we always celebrated the first night of Passover. To the youngest child capable of reading or singing the questions in Hebrew goes the honor of asking the four questions. In the mid-1960s that honor fell to me; at each seder I chanted the strange Hebrew words in my high-pitched child's voice.

I squirmed and slid on one of Nanny Fay's cushioned chairs, restless in my starched white shirt, fiddling with my clip-on tie. For the hundredth time, I wondered why I had to get dressed up for dinner at my grandparents' house. But my mother was adamant, so I tried not to pout as we went around the table, each reading a paragraph from the haggadah or special prayer booklet, alternating with my grandfather, the seder leader. When it was my turn, I pronounced the archaic English words, never stumbling, even when I didn't understand them—"For his mercy endureth for aye." Then it was Jerry's turn.

Jerry and my Aunt Terri struggled with the English pronunciation and the transliterated Hebrew prayers, reading haltingly, painfully. My uncle had had a Bar-Mitzvah, and memorized a bit of Torah for that special day many years ago, because he was a Jewish boy and that was what Papa Ben wanted. But Jerry was not the son my grandfather had hoped for.

Jerry's deafness was Papa's affliction as much as my uncle's, to have a son who could carry on the family name but couldn't quite pronounce it. Jerry read haltingly while we urged him on. My uncle's lips and tongue curled around the ancient text of the Passover story, his words guttural and deep, vowels skittering as if his mouth were full of marbles.

Before dinner, we read almost every page of our haggadahs, Papa leading the ritual in his practiced manner, his voice as worn as his face, a testament to ten thousand cigarettes and a hundred retellings of the ancient story. Sitting around the dining room table with my small family, the savory scents of Nanny Fay's Russian-Jewish cooking filtered through the room, lighter even than her renowned matzo balls. In my stiff white shirt and blue blazer, my neck crimped by my top button and that damned tie, I shifted from one position to another. My stomach gurgled, unsatisfied by small tastes of matzo and charoset, a mixture of apples, nuts, red wine and cinnamon.

The seder plate, metallic blue inlaid with gold, sat in the center of my grandmother's table with the ritual foods of Passover. There was a shank bone—traditionally from a lamb, but Nanny used a chicken. There was parsley, charoset, and horseradish or "Jewish Dristan," as Papa called it, since it immediately cleared one's nasal passages. Finally, there was an egg and a bowl of salt water in which the egg was dipped, to represent the tears of the Jewish slaves in Egypt.

Just before it was time to eat, my grandfather nodded in my direction. Picking up his cue, I launched into the tribal sounds of our ancient language. "Ma nishtanah halailah hazeh, mekol haleylot," I began, asking the adults, in the ritualized way Jewish boys had been asking for centuries, 'Why is this night different from all other nights?' In the winding melody I'd memorized at temple, I chanted each question, to the admiring eyes and sympathetic ears of my family. Then, reading responsively, the adults took turns answering the questions I'd asked.

My father smiled from across the table, his face flushed from the syrupy-sweet Manischewitz wine and pride in his middle son, while Papa nodded his approval. I exhaled, relieved my task was over, adrenalin pulsing through my body.

Finally, it was time to eat. We put our blue booklets aside as my grandmother passed around white china bowls of her special soup, the airy matzo balls half-immersed in chicken broth. This was followed by brisket, the beef marinated for hours, bathed in gravy and served in my Nanny's white-and-blue Corningware, accompanied by my mother's yams with marshmallow casserole. Cutlery clinked, and conversation burbled among us like a stream, the words circling around the island of my aunt and uncle.

Jerry and Terri ate methodically, looking around and then down, instead of at the fast-moving lips of the family. It was too difficult to catch up, being deaf in a group of hearing people—like the "pickle in the middle" in a schoolyard game.

Later, after the main course and dessert, the adults sipped their coffee and ate soft yellow pound cake (technically forbidden since it contained yeast), and my mother and grandmother retired to the kitchen to begin the massive clean up. Then my grandfather smiled slyly, and sent my two brothers, my cousin Sue and me to find the afikommen. This special piece of matzo from the seder table is hidden by the seder leader and then found or ransomed for a special reward. Once we'd found the matzo, wrapped in a cloth napkin, our grandfather would "redeem" it for a silver dollar, an exotic treat worth much more than its face value, a gift he gave to each child. Then we, the boys and men of the family, along with my other aunt and grandmother and my cousin, would sit around and finish the seder, stuffed with food, the adults mellowed by wine, liberally skipping pages.

As we neared the last line, "Next year in Jerusalem!" my mother and Nanny Fay re-joined us. We celebrated the end of the festive meal by singing "Chad Gad Ya," a silly Aramaic song about a man who bought a kid (or baby goat) "for two zuzim," a sort of Passover "Twelve Days of Christmas," each verse ending with the refrain, "Chad Gad Ya, Chad Gad Ya!"

Then, finally, we truly reclined. Released to play hide-and-seek with my cousin, I discarded my blazer and yanked off the tie. Papa Ben loosened his belt and lay back on Nanny's plastic-covered couch. My father, in those early years before he quit smoking, pulled out his pipe with its cherry-flavored tobacco and puffed away, content. Meanwhile, Jerry and Terri turned away from the table, watching Sue, and talking with each other in low tones.

Too soon it was time to leave. I kissed Papa's cheek, rough like the sandpaper in my father's workshop. His day-old growth of beard tickled my lips as he tousled my hair with his tobacco-stained fingers. I hugged Nanny Fay and warily approached my uncle. He pulled me in for a hug, impossibly tall, and lifted me off the ground, squeezing to just before it hurt.

I waved goodbye and walked toward my father's car for the quick one-mile ride home. I'd see my grandparents in a week or two, but might not see Jerry for several months, until the next family gathering. Still, he filled a space in my subconscious mind, a space in which I knew we were both different and yet somehow the same.

Chapter 7

Intersections

Today, many years after Jerry's death, I'm piecing together the details of my uncle's life, and the resonance between his experience as a deaf man among hearing people and my life as a gay man in a largely straight world. In retrospect, we both spent tremendous energy trying, and ultimately failing, to fit into the mainstream. My uncle's greatest success came through sports and hands-on activities, tinkering with machinery, drawing. Those were the same activities where I inevitably came up short.

Jerry was graceful and cat-like. While I also loved to dance, I lacked my uncle's smooth moves and his comfort with machinery. I knew instinctively that learning to drive would be an uphill battle, and that my fear would build and circle in on itself. I'd stumbled through other passages mastered by the boys around me—leaving the safety of home for the world of kindergarten; trying and failing to play team sports, and running away from the neighborhood bully.

My car accident seemed to set the tone for what came next. I was a fearful child, always teetering on the edge of humiliation. Afraid to defend myself, I was tormented for years by that doughy boy who chased me from our middle school bus stop. Like my emotions, my body betrayed me, too, stubbornly resisting adolescence long after my peers had sprouted body hair and muscles, their voices deepening, as I carried on in my high-pitched girlish squeak. When I reached high school, my friends towered above me. They stood 5'9" or more while I waited for deliverance at 5'4."

Jerry grew late, too. My mother claimed he was quite short when he was 15 and she went off to college. When she returned home the next summer, Jerry stood over six feet tall.

At 16, Jerry decided he wanted to go to Cleveland Heights High School with his hearing friends from the neighborhood, rather than to Shaw High in East Cleveland, with its oral program for deaf children. But Heights High had no facilities for deaf students. At first, Jerry was denied admission. According to family lore, my grandfather made an appointment to see the governor down in Columbus. Somehow, through the governor or an aide, Papa forced the school to accept Jerry as a student; within a few years, several other deaf students had enrolled at Heights High, too.

In the late 1940s, it was difficult for a deaf person to get a driver's license, even though the deaf are generally excellent drivers, their visual acuity and well-honed peripheral vision compensating for their inability to hear. Today there are few driving restrictions on deaf people.

Jerry learned to drive as he learned most everything else—by observing and getting the rhythm in his body, by doing it. Papa worked constantly, and had little time or patience to teach him. Besides, Jerry could hardly watch Papa's mouth, tucked under a wispy mustache, and concentrate on the road ahead. Instead, Papa found a professional instructor to teach my uncle.

By then Jerry may have realized that Papa, who knew so much, was a terrible driver, absent-minded and distracted, his mind still at the store or mulling over a story from that morning's Plain Dealer.

Jerry's cousin Jenny remembered the "big deal" made when he earned his driver's license. Soon after, Papa bought Jerry a used car, and he began driving several miles from his home in Cleveland Heights to his tutor's house in Shaker Heights for their twice-weekly sessions.

I picture Jerry driving a late 1940's-model Chevrolet, blue or black—the type favored by my grandfather. There, in the cavernous sedan, Jerry shifted smoothly into third and fourth gear, skirted the Shaker Lakes, and rolled under a canopy of elm trees, the engine humming beneath him. The gearshift became an extension of his body, arms and legs melding with machine, fine-tuned and efficient.

Over time, Jerry developed a fascination with the automobile. Years later, he would take his 6-year-old daughter, perched on his lap and several phone books, for rides around Cleveland, even letting her take the wheel as he called out the makes and models in his deaf speech—Pontiac Bon-ne-ville, Chevrolet Cor-vair—as if he were imparting some ancient wisdom.

Maybe, in the comfort of his car—eventually, it would be a chocolate-brown 1964 Chevy Impala, practical but not sporty—Jerry felt a sense of control he rarely felt anywhere else, a place where his deafness didn't really matter.

•

I counted down the days, sure that in spite of my terror, I could pass the written portion of my test and earn my temporary driving permit on my 16th birthday. I scoured the State of Ohio drivers' handbook as I had the Torah portion for my Bar-Mitzvah, memorizing obscure laws, and taking multiple-choice tests until I was confident I could pass on the first try. On February 27, 1973, my mother drove me to the State Highway Patrol headquarters in Mayfield Heights east of Cleveland, where I zipped through the test in 10 minutes, earning a score of 90. Now I was free to take my four on-the-road lessons at Heights Driving School, sit through several evening classes on driver's safety, and get my license.

My friend Dave's birthday was two days after mine. Tall, lean, and athletic, Dave was a younger version of my uncle on a narrower frame. We studied the driver's manual together, but Dave quickly left me behind, passing his road test just a week after his birthday. He'd been driving his sister's car around the neighborhood for two years; no one had to teach him the mechanics of driving.

One day in March, Dave ran home after our morning classes. Five minutes later, he pulled into the high school's driveway in his sister's fire-engine-red Dodge Challenger convertible. Dave and I had made plans to go to McDonald's during our lunch period once he passed his test. Now, as we rode down Interstate-271 toward Mayfield Heights, top down on an unseasonably warm day, I grooved to Dobie Gray's "Drift Away" on the car radio.

Even at 70 mph, Dave's smooth, supple arm rested lightly on the steering wheel, relaxed and masterful. I'd memorized the details of his face and body while daydreaming in Spanish class. His features—high forehead, dark almond-shaped eyes, smooth lips, and lean muscularity—reminded me of Yul Brynner in "The King and I," and awakened feelings I both savored and dreaded.

Soon after my birthday, I began my driving lessons. The older man who took me out remained calm, despite my bumping curbs and skirting tree-lawns. Thankfully, the instructor had a master-brake pedal, which saved us from several minor collisions. I needed lots of practice and more instruction. Unfortunately, my father had paid for only four sessions with a professional. Then I was left with my parents.

They replaced my instructor's greatest asset—patience—with anger, frustration, and a touch of hysteria. My Dad and I sat in Mom's hulking Mercury Monterrey, a four-door, six-passenger sedan. On the vinyl bench seat, my father squirmed as I pulled into traffic, yelled in alarm, and finally burst out with, "Jesus Christ, you're gonna get us both killed!" Soon we were engaged in our version of a Chinese fire drill, as Dad ordered me to get out, we circled round, and he replaced me in the driver's seat.

My mother was no better; she chewed her fingernails, sighed, and gasped, "Watch out!" as I neared a curb or strayed ever so slightly toward the yellow line. Still, a month later, I was avoiding curbs and oncoming traffic on a regular basis. Anxious to keep up with Dave, I scheduled my driving test for the following week.

42

The morning of my test was slate-gray and snowy. My stomach quivered as I stared out the window, thinking it was just my luck to face an April snowstorm. My mother picked me up at school that afternoon and pointed the Monterrey toward Highway Patrol headquarters. Soon I was behind the wheel, a buzz-cut patrolman riding shotgun. The officer held a clipboard in his meaty hands, prepared to rate my performance.

"Turn left," he said. I did, too anxious to wait for the oncoming car that technically had the right of way. The officer pointed out my mistake, shook his head, and made a notation on his clipboard. I felt panic rise in my chest, certain I'd failed. But the test continued as I circled the block and made it back to home base without further incident. Then I banked smoothly into a rectangular space defined by four large poles, a shade bigger than my mother's car. At least I'd passed the parallel-parking portion of the test.

I went inside the fluorescent-lit office and someone handed me a score-sheet. My jaw dropped; I'd passed—90 on the driving/95 on parallel parking. I was a legal driver in the State of Ohio.

Despite my fear, I wanted to impress my friends and not have to rely on my parents for rides. So, a few days later, I picked up Jim and Kevin and piloted my mother's Mercury to our Junior Achievement meeting in Cleveland Heights. I carefully drove the five-mile route to the JA center. Everything went according to plan until it was time to leave. Driving out of the parking lot, I misjudged the car's width and scraped the passenger side against a metal gate.

I dropped off my friends, my heart hammering, and went to face my father, who stomped out to the garage to inspect the car, and told me how "disappointed" he was in me. Still, I was allowed to take the car out again.

Over the next two years, several accidents followed. I covered up a minor one, paying $300 to a neighbor's maid after I dented her fender while pulling out of a friend's driveway. I had a more serious mishap on the way to senior prom at a friend's high school, but there were no injuries, and I managed to continue on to the party after confessing to my parents, who were surprisingly forgiving.

By the time I turned 18, I was almost 6' tall. My voice deepened, and I felt a bit less anxious behind the wheel. Soon I'd move on to other passages, other challenges, which would prove even more difficult than learning to drive.

Chapter 8

Good Vibrations

Cleveland Heights, Ohio
September 1952

Jerry walked into the social hall of Cleveland Heights High School, a head or two taller than the teenagers around him, a man among boys and girls. The hall, with its blond-wood floor and picture windows, had opened shortly before he graduated, in 1951. His cousin Jenny, a foot shorter and six years Jerry's junior at 16, trailed behind him, her strawberry brown hair bouncing as she walked. Miss Walters, the gray-haired Dean of Women, monitoring the crowd for hoods and thugs, smiled at Jerry, whom she remembered from his student days, and waved them into the room.

He looked back at Jenny, a girl he'd known since the day she was born. By the age of three or four, she could understand his speech, as he could follow hers. Instinctively, she knew to face him and to speak slowly, so he could read her lips. Unlike Jerry's father or his friends in the neighborhood, Jenny never got impatient or frustrated with him. Now Jerry waited for her, watching as she wove her way through the crowd behind him, as they headed front and center, toward the stage. There, half-hidden behind a stack of 45s and old 78 LPs, was a disc-jockey, outfitted in a white sports coat and red bow tie, who bounced between two turntables set up on a long cafeteria table, a speaker on either side.

Jerry, or Jinx as she thought of him, crooked a long finger and motioned her over. It was here, near the DJ and the speakers where he liked to dance, the bass rhythms of boogie-woogie streaming up from the floor and into his long legs. As she approached, his broad shoulders staked out space for them to dance.

Jerry tapped his feet, brown loafers half-obscured by gray-pleated pants set off against a navy blue V-neck sweater. Jenny was a latter-day bobby-soxer, with a white blouse and matching sox. Her poodle skirt fell below the knee, long enough to cover her crinoline petticoats and burgundy loafers, the heels torn off for extra "cool." Veterans—who'd danced together since Jenny was a girl of 8 and Jerry a boy of 14—they started slow and smooth, heating up as the music shifted from a ballad, "Heart and Soul" by The Four Aces, to up tempo swing, Red Foley's new hit, "Chattanoogie Shoeshine Boy."

Soon it was time for the dance contest. Several younger teachers circulated among the dancers taking notes, along with a few girls from the dance committee, wallflowers that seldom danced. Fifty couples jitterbugged to the beat, moved to the rhythm, the swishing stirring stomp of a hundred feet on wood.

The groups and the lyrics meant nothing to Jerry; it was the beat that called him. A one, two, three and they were off, Jenny following his lead, rock-step back, step forward, open and closed positions, and then a sweetheart turn into their signature "yo-yo move" as Jerry spun her out and back, and they became a single moving being, feet sliding skirt flying and then she was up, airborne, her eyes level with his.

She was flying, laughing, lighter even than her 100 pounds. Soon she was perched side to side on his bent knee in the "sidecar," her legs up again, right and then left. The other couples, bound by the laws of gravity, moved aside. They were in the zone, the place where music receded until they were floating in a rhythm without words.

A few old favorites came on, and the field was whittled down to ten couples, then five. Finally, the Andrew Sisters' "Boogie Woogie Bugle Boy" began, with its trademark trumpet call. Jerry and Jenny faced each other smiling as she fell back, bounced up, as Jerry spun her into a sweetheart move. Then they promenaded, strolling front and center. As the Sisters sang, "went out and drafted the band," Jenny was airborne once more, over Jerry's back and then somehow on her feet again, facing him.

Dimly she heard them clapping—the teachers, the girls on the dance committee, the other couples—and the smile on Jerry's face was worth more to her than the blue ribbons, more even than the furtive looks of the other boys who longed to dance with her, if they ever got the chance.

Chapter 9

Dancing Machine

Cleveland, Ohio
June 1975

We streamed through the door of the club, decked out in tight shirts that emphasized our narrow teenage waists, stovepipe pants, puffed up hairstyles. Natural fabrics were not in vogue; it was the age of polyester and flammable materials. I fit right in, with my shoulder-length brown hair and plaid bellbottoms. It was my shoes that stood out.

The Agora, a famed nightclub near Cleveland State University, attracted rockers from Paul Simon to ZZ Top. On this night the club was transformed into a disco, with a Plexiglas floor that lit up in time to the music and a disco ball above the dancers, all set up for the first night of our prom. The club opened early for our private gathering and, though no alcohol was served, I'd soon grow intoxicated from the pulsing beat, the rhythm and blues music, and my gyrations on the dance floor.

I'd bought those red shoes the year before, when as a high school junior I'd finally reached puberty. At 16, I had almost given up hope of ever making the transition from boy to man, and of growing taller than 5'4", though I'd been told that men in my family grew late. When my latent hormones kicked in, my mother took me to Value City, a down at the heels discount store known for good prices and bad atmosphere in working-class Warrensville Heights. There I discovered a pair of platform shoes with thick two-inch heels the color of blood. I simply had to have them, even though the rest of my wardrobe was tame by '70s standards, a collection of brown, blue, and gray.

By June of my senior year, I stood about 6′2″ in those platform shoes and weighed 135 pounds. Though I was too thin—I couldn't seem to put on weight no matter how I tried—it felt good to be breathing the rarefied air of my taller friends, the ones who had towered over me since their growth spurts at 13 or 14, while I waited and prayed that I wouldn't follow in my 5′2″ mother's tiny footsteps.

My prom date was my girlfriend Randi, a sophomore with large hazel eyes and thick eyelashes. Her olive skin and those eyes, which reflected the light around her, seemed exotic and vaguely Middle Eastern, though her forbears were Eastern European Jews like mine. Randi was a good girl, an A-student and a future accountant. In our year together, we did little more than neck and pet; I felt no pressure to go further. Randi liked to dance, and for reasons I couldn't quite fathom, she liked me as well. Perhaps because I was a "nice boy," one her parents approved of.

We filed in, couple by couple, along with our teacher-chaperones. The music started to play. Randi wore a light pink dress, her hair shoulder-length and dark brown. She had urged me to cut my hair, but I thought I looked cool with my red-brown locks falling toward my shoulders. Years later, scanning our prom picture, I wondered what I was thinking; I looked androgynous/half-girl, standing to the left of the real girl beside me.

Already, at 18, I chafed to leave the sheltered world of Beachwood, where everyone was related to everyone else, our grandparents' shtetl transplanted to the shores of Lake Erie. My girlfriend had no such desires. An only child, she was linked to her parents, wore their expectations like a cloak, heavy and comforting. I liked Randi, but couldn't imagine a future with her or anyone else in my small hometown.

Still, the weekend came as an escape, a reprieve from the past two months. For three full days, I could simply have fun, knowing that a week later I would officially graduate from Beachwood High. A few months later, I'd leave Cleveland for good.

The Agora's lights—red, purple, white—created a snapshot effect as we were frozen momentarily on the dance floor. I scanned the room. Kids I'd known since elementary school moved in slow motion. Most were acquaintances; a few were friends. And there were some in a vague middle ground—the boys I idolized—the lean muscled jocks who performed feats I couldn't imagine, like playing shortstop on the varsity baseball team or running track and reaching the state finals.

Chaka Khan and Rufus' funky "Tell Me Something Good" boomed out from the DJ's booth and brought me back into the moment. Though we didn't follow set dance steps, I had my signature moves, and Randi mirrored them, comfortable in her body as I was in mine, if only on the dance floor.

As Chaka sang the chorus—*Tell me something good/tell me that you like it, yeah, followed by a chorus of ooh-ah-oo-ah-ah*—a bass pant still vivid in my mind—I moved three steps to the right, three steps to the left. Each time I'd throw in my patented grapevine step—left foot over right as I moved to the right, then right over left as I went the other way, Randi following me, our fingers snapping as we got down on the Agora floor.

Next came the Bee Gees' "Jive Talking," *Jeh-Jeh-Jeh Jive talking*.........As the sweat trickled down my chest and stained my beige polyester shirt I did a half turn in my pimp-style shoes, rocking my shoulders to one side and then another, moving in synch with Randi until we almost became one. For a few moments, I could forget my life outside that room, forget Jerry's death and my father's betrayal.

Unlike my uncle, I didn't command the floor. No one stopped and admired my grapevine steps, the way I grooved to the music. No one but Randi paid me much attention. As the night went on my focus drifted to some of the athletic boys I admired. They too had thick hair, tight shirts and bellbottom pants, but wore them with so much more panache.

Randi smiled, flashing her long eyelashes, and headed for the powder room. I stood to one side of the dance floor, watching the Adonises move to the Doobie Brothers' "Black Water." Some were stiff and jerky, afraid to shed their protective cool. I was more fluid and natural on the dance floor, they more graceful where it mattered, on the athletic field and in the social whirl of high school.

By 11 pm, the dance was over. Soon the prom, and my last few days at Beachwood High would be over, too. It would be ten years before I'd see the objects of my teenage envy. By then they'd be gaining weight, losing their hair, no longer the stars they were in high school. By then, I'd be coming out and starting the next phase of my life, a chapter I would not share with them.

Part Two
The Geographic Cure

Chapter 10

Due Date 1975

On September 20, 1975 we packed up my father's gold Lincoln and headed west toward Evanston, Illinois. I'd waited with fear, excitement and mounting impatience for the day to come, watched with jealousy when my friends departed several weeks earlier. After the events of that spring and summer—Jerry's and Papa's deaths, my father's infidelity and my mother's sharing of the details, and the harsh reality of taking apart the drug store and watching Papa's life work dissolve before my eyes—I was ready to go.

And not. I'd always been a 'mama's boy,' and cried my way through three weeks of overnight camp the summer I was 12. It was my parents' idea, their decree that each of their sons should go (preferably far) away for the summer. This was my least-bad option, 21 days at Camp Wise, a Jewish "sleepaway" camp located only an hour from home in the countryside east of Cleveland. Those three weeks felt like six, doing the things a boy was supposed to enjoy as my brothers did—living in a tent with kids my own age, playing sports, getting lots of "fresh air" with my compatriots. My focus was on survival, trying to avoid humiliation on the ball field (impossible), a canoe trip (unlikely) and even in the dining hall where the observant kids knew the motzi (blessing) chanted before every meal and even after three weeks I only had it half right, and knew I would never sing it again in my irreligious family, as I would never (God willing) return to overnight camp.

When I was home, my mother doted, worried, and complained about me in equal measure. I was told to go outside, "get out of my hair," find something else to do besides watching old black and white movies on Channel 43's "Dialing for Dollars" or reading one of her paperback romances. Yet somehow we were bound together, a tether that let me stray only so far.

The years passed slowly, gray and dark like the Cleveland winters. By junior year I'd found my niche, a way of navigating the currents of high school. I developed a small circle of friends, good boys who studied, obeyed their parents, held down part-time jobs and earned good grades. Sex was something for college and beyond, a relief for me, who feared it would be hard to fake what I did not feel.

Now I was escaping from my parents' house too, which felt so oppressive that last summer. In late July, after Papa died, I left for a three-week vacation. My father had offered me the use of his truck camper, so that my friend Kevin and I could celebrate our high school graduation with a road trip through the Northeast US and Canada. We'd planned the trip that spring, before Papa Ben's death, and by the time I left, my grandfather's store was empty, the dust settled.

After my string of minor accidents, the idea of piloting a full-sized pick-up and attached camper—my father's camper—made me queasy. But Kevin was a good driver and so I let him handle the fine movements—such as backing into camping spaces, which required the confidence and driving skills I lacked.

There was tension on that trip, a result of our close quarters, the two of us sleeping an arm's length apart above the truck-bed of my Dad's tan pickup. After the first week, I called home from an island in Lake Champlain, Vermont. I told my father I was lonely, as Kevin and I were barely speaking. Dad told me to stick it out; I really had no choice. The next day we got to Montreal and things shifted—and then shifted again. By the time we reached Cleveland we were silent again, each nursing our resentments against the other. I knew I was in the right; after all, Kevin and his sort-of-girlfriend, whom he had met the previous summer at a resort in the Catskills, (we were staying over with her parents outside of Montreal) had gone off on a date, leaving me alone with her little brother, a 13-year-old boy with more common sense than his 17-year-old sister.

Since the subway closed at 1 am, Alvin and I were careful to catch the train back to Laval, heeding the warning his parents had called out before we left for La Ronde, the great amusement park in the St. Lawrence River, a leftover from the 1967 World's Fair. We got back to Alvin's house on time, but Kevin and his girlfriend weren't there. I headed down to sleep in the basement. Soon after, the girl's parents got a call from their daughter—they'd jumped on the last bus out and were stranded in some dark corner of the city, an area of warehouses and abandoned buildings.

I heard her father cursing in Hungarian-flavored English as he ventured out at 2 am to god-knew-where on the far side of Montreal. A door slammed and I burrowed under the blankets and escaped into sleep. Sometime later I heard Kevin slide onto the mattress near mine. The next morning we said our goodbyes to the girl's mother—her father had thankfully gone to work—and drove toward Ottawa.

•

We emerged from our 3000-mile odyssey with our friendship teetering in the balance. But within a few weeks we'd put the trip behind us, focusing instead on our upcoming adventures at college—he at Miami University in tiny Oxford, Ohio, and me at Northwestern, just north of Chicago.

The trip had been a series of distractions and then I was back waiting that final, inexorable month after Kevin and my other friends had left, the black footlocker that had seen both my brothers to camp propped open in one corner of my bedroom, stuffed full of clothing weeks before my due date.

The drive to Chicago was predictable—my parents and I following our assigned scripts. My mother sat in the front passenger seat while my father drove, fast but carefully. At some point we passed through downtown, missed the turn to head north on the Dan Ryan expressway toward Evanston, and had to retrace our route. Dad complained about Mom's navigation, while she blamed him for not listening. I tried to distract them both by reading the directions out loud and pointing to the nearest entrance ramp.

As we neared the college something stirred in my abdomen, a mix of excitement and foreboding. I'd always lived under my parents' roof, had never been apart from them beyond those three-week stints at camp and in the truck camper, or when they took their one or two-week annual vacations without me. Now I'd be away for months at a time, the only connection a voice on the telephone on our weekly Sunday calls.

Soon we reached my dorm, a high-rise on the edge of campus. My father and I began carrying boxes, the two of us hoisting the footlocker into the elevator, while my mother began unpacking my clothes, getting things organized. Resting safely in my dorm room were corduroys in various shades of blue, maroon and gray, Carole King's Tapestry album and my other records, and the black polyester leisure suit my mother insisted I buy for college. The dormitory, a boxy brick apartment building, loomed over us as we emptied the car. If I craned my neck from my seventh-floor room, I could see a slice of the cool gray lake, as well as the modest house next door—headquarters of the Women's Christian Temperance Union—which had been founded a century earlier and had made Evanston a dry town, one that outlawed bars and watering holes.

I met my roommate Randall, who was not the white boy pictured in our freshman class booklet but rather a tall, toothy black kid from Memphis with medium brown skin, tortoise shell glasses and a picked out 'fro. (His photo had been switched with a white classmate from Escanaba, Michigan). I thought it was cool to have an African-American roommate—we had only 5 or 10 black students at Beachwood High School and I didn't know any of them well—but something else concerned me.

Randall was effeminate, in an 'out there' theater-major sort of way, and meeting him initially depressed me. This was too close to home, and brought up feelings I didn't want to ponder, not then, on the first day of my new life. Meanwhile, my parents and I headed over to the student union to get something to eat and explore the campus, which stretched along the shore of Lake Michigan. The setting was still beautiful, as it had been when I'd visited with two friends the previous fall, but now I felt hollow, unsettled by the prospect of my parents' departure and being left alone to live with Randall and two other boys I didn't know.

I stood off to one side and watched them prepare to leave. My father was sweating circles under his polo shirt, as usual. He sweated profusely when he exerted himself, sat in a warm room, or even drank hot coffee. Dad had mellowed since his heart attack, but his impatience sparked around my mother and her need for attention. Now, his trunk emptied of my belongings, he was ready to go.

Glancing back at my mother, I noticed her eyes were wet, mascara threatening to run down her face. In the past four months, she had lost her father and her brother. Now, I was leaving, too. My father was probably still carrying on his affair, spending weekday nights away, mentally absent even when he was home. My brother Alex was practically living at his best friend's house. I felt a ball of tears move up from my abdomen, which I willed myself to contain. I'd been so anxious to leave, to free myself from the tension and sadness of that oppressive summer at home. Now I wondered how I'd manage, living with three strangers, packed into a dorm with hundreds more. I wondered, too, how my mother would cope without me.

My father emerged from the Mark IV, stuck out his hand and shook mine. Once again I felt his physical strength as he enveloped my smaller hand in his, and sensed his power, which existed in uneasy balance with his weakened heart. Then I walked to the passenger side and bent down to face my mother. The tears were gone; she had 'pulled herself together' for my benefit. I hugged her across the doorframe and felt her thin bones and the shallowness of her breath. A few feet away my father waited, his foot tapping impatiently on the floorboard.

"I'll talk to you soon," I said, my voice quavering.

"Call us on Sunday," my mother said. And they were gone, the Lincoln glinting in the setting sun as they headed west, my father at the wheel, in control.

I felt guilty leaving my mother, knowing that Dad was unfaithful and hadn't really supported her over those summer months — my assumptions colored by my mother's secret. The emotional constellation of their marriage was beyond me, a calculus I couldn't figure, like the mathematical formulas Dad sketched when he had tried, and failed, to explain Algebra to me a few years earlier.

I took my mother's side, felt my father's disloyalty to us, the family unit, which must be preserved because there is such a thing as right and wrong and isn't that what they—what he—taught me? Now he was just a middle-aged hypocrite who was afraid of dying and I understood some of that, because of the heart attack that almost killed him four years earlier, and now with Jerry's heart attack on my mother's side I knew my own clock was ticking, and that I shared their faulty genes.

The father I had before his heart attack was a rigid engineer who expected life to proceed in orderly fashion, his sons to follow his lead. My new Dad was looser, cooler, more inclined to let his hair down (in this case a comb-over sprayed into place). But I'd been raised by that first father and a mother who was high strung, who went into battle when a real crisis took place, who was always on call. When the battle was on she marshaled her ferocious energy and her will—she actually quit smoking when my father had his heart attack—and I was her sentry and watched her for signs of trouble, and there were many, mostly false alarms. Over those last months of my childhood there were real disturbances in our midst, and now we were confidants, allied in a silent pact against my Dad.

Still, on some level I knew my parents loved each other. Yes they bickered, but they were united by something—shared history, youth, first love—that I hoped would keep them together. They had met at Ohio University in remote Athens in the mid-1940s, still in their teens. I'd seen their old black and white home movies, in which my mother, who tipped the scale at 100 pounds, was chubby, her now stiff bouffant hair wild and unruly. Almost 30 years later, I sensed the threads that bound them together: the ritual morning kiss before my father headed out the door, the way he appraised my mother when they were going out on a Saturday night—pride and ownership—and the excitement in my mother's eyes when they turned to leave for their nights out, temporarily freed of her responsibilities and for now, holding his full attention. The scent of her L'air du Temps perfume, mixed with my father's Old Spice aftershave, lingered in the hallway as my father revved the Corvette's engine, as they headed off to a party or a banquet, an adult world I glimpsed only through the occasional photos that found their way into my mother's neatly printed albums.

My parents came from the same Cleveland-Jewish world and spoke the same language, even if the words got misconstrued or sometimes lost in the chasm that appeared between them like a fissure on dry ground. There were those 25 years of togetherness, my mother's steely determination to get through whatever obstacles life presented, and my father's drive to build a business and then to recover from the massive heart attack that brought him to his knees with Mom's support—that joined them together in a Jewish stew of love, obligation, and guilt on my father's part—mixed with a desire to live out the youth he'd surrendered by wedding at the tender age of 23.

And so they left me to my own devices. By then, neither Jerry nor Papa occupied much space in my conscious mind. I was too full of the new world of college, my doubts of where I might fit in, and behind it all, the state of my parents' marriage, and what would become of our family.

During fall term, I came to know my three roommates. Mark, a boy with Apollo's face on a blocky, hairy body, and who reminded me of the 1970s actor/heartthrob Perry King, was the consummate New Yorker, a confirmed cynic who trusted no one. Paul, a mellow pot-smoking WASP from Colorado, befriended Mark, as they shared their tales of sexual conquests and high school debauchery.

Meanwhile, Randall was the extrovert of our floor. Though I suspected he was gay, I focused on his kindness, humor, and general sense of fun rather than on his telltale mannerisms. A charismatic guy, Randall quickly gathered a group of theatre-major friends and hangers-on content to be in his shadow. By October, I'd joined Randall's entourage and moved into the front room of our suite, leaving Mark and Paul to bond in the back.

On Wednesday nights, Randall would "baby sit" for his cousins in Chicago. On one of those nights, Mark saw Randall slip into a silver Lincoln. "Randall's got a sugar daddy—you see all those fancy clothes he's got." I nodded dumbly when Mark explained that Randall had probably found a rich man to take care of him. I wondered if Mark had similar doubts about me, and if he thought I was gay, too.

During that first quarter of freshman year, my Freshman Comp professor was a young instructor with wire-rim glasses and curly black hair. Justin was cool; he insisted we call him by his first name. He wore a silver band on his left hand and bulky wool sweaters. A lean, fit-looking man of 30, he warned us of the workload we'd be facing in his class, now that we were no longer "big fish in the little pond of high school."

Our first paper was due four weeks into the semester—four to six pages, typed. An essay on Sherwood Anderson's Winesburg, Ohio—an 1890's small-town Midwest far removed from the suburban Cleveland I knew, and totally irrelevant to my life in the 1970s, or so I thought. Forty years later, I recall the essence of that first assignment. Many of us had been academic stars in our small high schools. Northwestern would be different—we'd be ranked over a curve; most of us could expect C's rather than A's. If his intention was to scare me, he succeeded brilliantly.

I was afraid of the typewriter, and wondered if I could write a college-level paper. Once I 'hit my stride,' I typed a page an hour, using half a bottle of Wite-Out in the process. My gold Smith-Corona portable sat on my narrow desk, humming, waiting for me to pick up the tune. I felt electric current pass through my hands. A worn copy of Winesburg rested in my lap as I looked over Justin's directions. Fine tune what you have to say—I want a main idea, supporting statements and a summary of your key points. It is time you learn what college writing is all about. And don't get too hung up on this first paper—do your best and expect the worst. You'll have four more chances to bring up your grade.

Anderson's short stories made me edgy. The first piece, "Hands," was about a twitchy former schoolteacher who went by the name of Wing Biddlebaum. As I read it, my gut tightened in recognition. Wing, whose real name was Adolph Myers, had been forced out of a small Pennsylvania town because he couldn't keep his hands to himself. While his affectionate caresses appeared innocent, "a half witted boy became enamored of the young master." "In his bed at night he [the boy] imagined unspeakable things." Other boys came forward to accuse the young teacher of touching them. Adolph fled for his life, came to live with an elderly aunt in Winesburg, and took the name Wing Biddlebaum, his former life a secret. After his aunt died, Wing lived alone and kept to himself. A gifted field hand and an eccentric, Wing was known in town only for the fluttering of his hands.

There was no evidence that Wing had shared anything but platonic touch with his students. But I knew Wing was gay. And I, too, like the half-witted boy in Anderson's story, imagined "unspeakable things," wrestling in my fantasies with several handsome young men I saw on campus. I'd escaped from Cleveland to suburban Chicago, but my suppressed desire had come along for the ride.

The essay flowed out of me. I don't remember the argument I made, or my analysis of Wing's character and Anderson's reasons for creating him. What remained beyond that term was only the satisfaction of earning an A in the course, and beneath that, a palpable fear that my own shameful secret would be discovered.

Chapter 11

A Man with a Plan

Sitting in the new Communicative Disorders building on the north end of campus on a cool fall day in 1975, I studied my classmates. Most of them were sorority girls majoring in speech pathology or audiology, two fields that seemed painfully dry compared to the excitement and drama of teaching deaf children. The girls dressed alike and traveled in packs, wearing the same preppy clothes their mothers might have worn a generation earlier. As fall turned toward winter they sported matching sweaters—gray, pale yellow, light blue with half-circle floral designs, laurels beneath their pale necks. Beyond those girls, with their fair skin and hair (I remember them as all blonde, all WASP), there were the "unaffiliated" types like me, who were not part of the Greek system and didn't want to be, and the locals—commuter students who lived at home with their parents and had a tenuous connection to campus life.

There were few other men in my "com dis" courses. Those who did show up followed the sorority girls into speech pathology or audiology, research-oriented fields considered more scientific and prestigious than teaching. Over the course of the year, I'd sit in the library, skimming articles about articulation and speech defects in hearing children, and wonder, what, if anything, this had to do with my future career. Though I felt insecure about my masculinity and sexuality, I didn't mind being the only man in my program. Unlike some of my classmates, I had a clear sense of my vocation.

I spent hours, weeks, months, among those girls in a series of technical courses, based on the "medical model" approach to deaf education dominant at the time. Deaf children, like those with cleft palates or learning disabilities, had problems to be addressed. The deaf had no natural language or culture to speak of, even though American Sign Language had finally been recognized by linguists and researchers as a complex language that could express the full range of human thought. Instead the deaf were viewed as handicapped, in need of repair.

During my first two years at Northwestern I slogged through Introduction to Audiology, Acoustics (the physics of sound) and Phonetics, learning what I would quickly forget, with no place to apply my newfound knowledge after the classes ended. I spent many hours in Northwestern's speech clinic, observing through one-way glass as junior and senior Speech Pathology majors tutored little children in the fine art of articulation.

"No, Bobby," they'd say, "Say pat, puh-puh-puh pat, now buh-buh-buh-bat." Those kids were clearly as bored as I was. I squirmed along with them as I noted each future therapist's strategies, writing down the same thing in different words, knowing I would never work as a speech pathologist, would rather go back to my part time job in crowd control at Sea World of Ohio.

In my Phonetics class, I sat with a few of my 'deaf-ed' major friends, listening to an outsized woman named Hilda Fisher. Dr. Fisher had written the leading textbook in the field of Phonetics. She had also developed a system of transcription to identify and record the sounds of human speech. We all felt intimidated by Dr. Fisher, who reminded me of Julia Child, with the same excellent diction and clipped speech, except that she focused on speech production instead of cooking.

Every Friday, Dr. Fisher gave us a quiz in which we had to transcribe a series of spoken words using phonetic symbols. As the weeks flew by she seemed less threatening and more encouraging. Or perhaps we'd simply been trained to do as we'd been told, and had mastered her system. Eventually I earned an A in the course, accumulating a vast storehouse of obscure knowledge in the process.

In my first-year classes, I learned to interpret an audiogram and to identify a phoneme—the sound units that make up human speech. I had a plan and could see it all unfolding—me, the male version of Anne Sullivan in The Miracle Worker, my hands arcing through the air, conveying knowledge to my deaf students, receptive sponges who would soak up whatever I had to give them.

Finally, in my sophomore year, I got to take "Sign Language." Strangely, there were only one or two sign language courses in the Deaf Education program at Northwestern. Still, I was thrilled to finally be using my hands, if only in one or two-sign sentences.

A hearing professor taught our class; there were no deaf instructors in the program. Each week we were given a list of English vocabulary words and their corresponding signs. It wasn't until much later, when I was teaching at the Ohio School for the Deaf and studying American Sign Language with a deaf teacher, that I came to understand that English words and ASL signs don't have a 1-1 word/sign correspondence. Learning sign, I'd figure out years later, meant using it in context, embedded in a phrase, sentence or message.

What I was really learning at Northwestern was a jumble of English signs grafted onto ASL, a convoluted system designed to fit spoken English. This system, developed by hearing teachers of the deaf, was called "Total Communication." The developers claimed that deaf children would benefit from getting speech and sign simultaneously. But the system, I realized years later, didn't work. You can't speak English and sign in ASL. When speaking English, the signs naturally follow English word order and don't make visual sense; ASL and English have very different systems of grammar. We were simply producing visual noise. Meanwhile, I naively assumed I was learning the language of deaf people, and that in a few short years I would be ready to teach.

Chapter 12

Summer of '77

I was in a used bookstore in Jacksonville, Florida when I saw it. The store was huge, cavernous, and I wandered around aimlessly until I noticed a handmade sign titled Sign Language on my right. I turned and there, for the first time in almost 40 years, I saw a thick yellow paperback titled *Signing Exact English* on a shelf facing me. The book was labeled 1980 edition, but it looked identical to the one I received in the summer of 1977, when I volunteered as a teacher's aide in a class for primary school-aged deaf children in San Francisco.

I'd gone to the Bay Area ostensibly to explore a new city, to earn college credit, and to do something productive with my summer off. But on another level I was running away, going as far as I could within the continental US. (I'd spent the previous summer at my parents' house in Cleveland, and swore I would not make the same mistake twice.) Pressed up against the Pacific Ocean in that iconic, romantic city, I hoped to leave my self-doubt behind, to have a series of adventures, and to live the life of a normal college student.

Most of my fellow students in Northwestern University's summer program found internships in public agencies, working at city hall or in the courts. I was the only one who planned to teach, but I quickly found a position working with an energetic twenty-something teacher in the San Francisco Public Schools named Carolyn. Soon I was using the minimal sign language I'd absorbed in my single class at Northwestern, along with vocabulary from the "SEE book" that turned out to be my bible during the two months I worked there.

The book featured 400 pages of large black and white illustrations, pairing signs with their English words in a one to one correspondence, and alphabetized from A to Z. Much later, I would discover that ASL signs usually have multiple meanings depending on their context. In addition, many of the signs were initialized in the SEE system, to supposedly make the words easier for deaf students to understand. For example, the SEE sign for 'kid' was the letter k under one's nose, rather than the natural sign used in ASL, the little and index fingers jutting out as the hand passed below the nostrils, as if wiping a runny nose. By the 1990s, SEE signs had fallen out of use, and deaf adults generally reverted to their natural tongue, American Sign Language. (The Deaf community never embraced SEE, with its artificial signs and English grammatical structure). But in the '70s, almost any form of sign language was considered progressive by hearing teachers of the deaf—as opposed to the oral approach that had dominated deaf education for decades—and I was thrilled to get the book, to interact with deaf children, and to put my plan of becoming a teacher into motion).

My summer odyssey began on the drive west with two other Northwestern students. I'd gone home to Cleveland for a brief visit, and then flew back to Chicago to meet Ray and Steve, both rising juniors like me. Ray and his wealthy Italian-American family lived outside Chicago, and we were taking his car on the journey, from Chicago's northern suburbs to San Francisco by way of Omaha, Denver, and Elko, Nevada—a random stopping point along the way where we were escorted out of a casino for making a racket after we hit a small jackpot on a slot machine—and San Jose. We reached San Francisco at the end of June and bedded down temporarily with two other students who had rented a ratty first floor apartment at 151 Hartford Street in the Castro district that spring. In Denver, Steve and Ray met and romanced two local college girls, while I headed off to our shared room alone. Later that night, I woke up while the guys whispered their conquests and wondered if I was gay. I closed my eyes in the darkness and fell back into restless sleep. For the rest of the trip, I tried to allay their doubts and be one of the boys, but when we reached San Francisco they pointedly searched for a two-bedroom apartment without me. I ended up staying on Hartford Street, where the current tenants needed another body to cover the rent.

Our apartment was redolent of dog, the air thick and weighty even with the windows open. Layers of dust and hair were caked to the worn couch, the ratty chairs, adhering to the fading wallpaper and kitchen counters. One of the previous tenants, who had left a month before I arrived, had an older dog and her 10 puppies. Though the dogs were gone, their fur and odor remained a constant throughout the summer, though the smell did fade over time, or perhaps I simply grew used to it.

There were other sights and scents in the neighborhood. While I knew that San Francisco was a mecca for gay men, one of the few places in the country were they could live openly, I hadn't planned to live among them. But the Castro turned out to be the epicenter of gay culture, with many cheap and rundown apartments those young men and students like me could afford. And so I ended up just a block off Castro Street in the heart of the gay neighborhood, a place perfectly designed to stoke the fear and desire that had haunted me back at Northwestern.

On our first night in town, worn out from the road but energized by the lights and rhythm of the city, I walked down Castro Street with Ray, Steve, and my new roommates. Men spilled out of the bars; I'd soon come to recognize the "clone" look popular in the Castro. White-T shirts or form-fitting flannel, skin-tight Levis, with keys and kerchiefs displayed in a particular semaphore I never deciphered, which signified whether they were 'tops,' 'bottoms,' or into other activities. The outfit might be topped off with a jean or leather jacket, faces framed with a mustache and sideburns. Those men seemed to be going for a hyper-masculine look—and on that night, one drunk muscleman of about 40, with buzz-cut hair and Popeye-sized biceps, followed the five of us across Market Street, threatening to "kick our asses" as we walked on, morphing into the scared young boys we were.

We arrived in San Francisco just before the July 4th holiday, and as I watched the fireworks explode over one of the city's many hills, showering the Victorians below with colored light, I felt a sense of promise in this place where anything seemed possible. I'd reached the far shore, a place where the accepted rules of behavior didn't apply. Yet I felt enormous pressure to fit in, not with the gay men of the Castro, but with my roommates, my classmates, my peers. Still, it was hard not to notice that the certainties were falling away, that the world around me was whipsawed by change, no more stable than the ground under our feet.

Patty Hearst—the kidnapped heiress who had sided with her captors—had just received five years' probation in a sensational-ized trial. The San Francisco Chronicle, which I read each morning before trooping off to school, was filled with other disquieting stories that echoed the uncertainty in my own life. Reading Herb Caen's columns about life in the city, I learned about Jim Jones and the People's Temple, a cult that had flourished in San Francisco; by the summer of 1977 most of his followers had followed the false prophet into the jungles of Guyana, where he created the settlement of Jonestown. Many of those followers, along with Jones himself, would die in a suicide pact the next year.

Meanwhile, at our weekly seminars, when the 20 students in my program came together to talk about their internships, I heard about infighting in city government, tension between conserva-tives and progressives like Mayor Moscone. (In the fall of 1978, Dan White, a conservative ex-police officer and former councilman, would kill Moscone and the first gay council member, Harvey Milk, at city hall.)

Other cults flourished in the area, too, as I learned first hand. Twice in the space of three days I was approached by "Moonies," followers of the South Korean cult leader Sun Myung Moon, who had a strong base in the Bay Area. My roommate Greg, who worked at city hall, told me about the Moonies' modus operandi. Typically they approached teenagers and young adults and tried to lure them to dinner, eventually coercing them to retreat centers out east, where they were cut off from friends and family and essentially brainwashed into joining the group. Once, on my way home from downtown, I was accosted by a boy about my age, who struck up a conversation and invited me to dinner with a group he called the "Creative Community." After a few minutes I begged off, explaining that I was late for a meeting.

A few days later, I was on my way to the Greyhound Bus Station and a quick trip to Santa Cruz for a weekend at the beach with my other roommate, Phil. As I zigged and zagged through the Friday crowds on Market Street, I was brought up short by a boy of about 18, with long stringy hair, and an older woman in her 20s. The boy, with eyes that seemed a bit out of focus, asked me where I was from, where I was going, and how long I'd been in the area. The woman said little, but kept her eyes fixed on my face. I was holding a small duffel bag with my clothing for the weekend, and as the boy droned through his canned speech— I got another invitation to a potluck at the Creative Community—the woman felt up my bag; perhaps she was looking for drugs or money. I tucked the duffel into my body, told them I was late for my bus, and scurried away, afraid they might follow me. Soon I was swallowed by the crowd, and they moved on to another potential victim.

Sometime later, I read an article in the Chronicle, which described the process by which the "Moonies" recruited new members, often young, lonely travelers who lacked a support system in the area. It was obvious that I'd been targeted, the perfect mark. Beyond San Francisco, life seemed no less tranquil. The "Son of Sam" murders riled New York City, while Anita Bryant fanned the flames of anti-gay bigotry across the nation, overturning Miami's gay rights ordinance in the process. In August, Elvis Pressley, an icon of my 1960s childhood—though my friends and I regarded him as something of a joke—died, followed a few days later by Groucho Marx.

Over time, I learned my way around the Castro, no longer physically afraid of the men who streamed out of the bars, the clothing stores, the 24-hour donut shop. Instead I was frightened by what they represented—that I might be bent, like them. I confronted those fears not only in the street, but inside my apartment, too. Greg was a high school wrestler, sinewy and lean, with wavy blond hair and hazel eyes. Quiet, laid-back and self-assured, he projected a quiet confidence that may have come from his high school exploits, his Southern California roots, and his easy grace with women. Greg had a job at city hall that grew out of his spring internship, though I never figured out exactly what he did there. He was, however, well-placed to secure marijuana from a contact he'd acquired at his workplace. For the first and only time in my college career, I smoked with Greg and Phil on a weekly basis. The pot, which I'd smoke via Greg's pipe, made me hungry, sleepy, and just barely took the edge off the anxiety that ran through my body that summer, a silent current. After school, jazzed and restless, I might come home and cook my one specialty, spaghetti with tomato sauce. From Greg, I learned the trick of throwing a noodle on our kitchen wall—if it stuck, the pasta was ready to eat. Later, after getting high, we'd run through a box of Wheat-thins and I'd stumble off to bed, visions of Greg's muscular chest cycling through my mind.

At the school where I was working as a teacher's aide I watched Carolyn, the quintessential young California blonde, with her long straight brown hair, tanned skin, wire-rim glasses and fluid signs, as she managed the 10 deaf children in her class, escorting them to the San Francisco Aquarium, the Zoo, and Golden Gate Park. Back in the classroom, she gave them each a children's cookbook with easy to follow recipes. After observing her for several weeks, I was given the chance to teach the kids how to make butter from cream, shaking the pints of cream until the liquid thickened into butter. That relatively simple lesson, delivered in a combination of Signing Exact English and gesture, was the highlight of my internship. Slowly, I picked up more signs from the kids, but I was choppy rather than fluid, and wondered if I'd ever become a skilled teacher like Carolyn. Still, I was determined to try.

After a day at school, I'd exit the streetcar at Market and Castro and walk toward our odorous apartment. Twin Peaks, an iconic bar with curving picture windows that displayed rows of men looking both outward to the street and at each other in a '70s tableau, stood at that busy intersection, the pulsing music of that summer — Thelma Houston's "Don't Leave Me This Way" and The Emotions' "Best of My Love" thrumming as I walked by, along with a cloud of smoke that trailed the men streaming in and out of the bar. Next came the Castro Theater, a down at the heels remnant of a golden age, where I saw my first Marx Brothers movie, "Duck Soup," and the all day/all night donut shop, which seemed to draw even more customers than Twin Peaks. Around the corner, as I turned left on 17th, there was a store called All American Boy, which sold T-shirts, jeans and undies for the well-dressed clone, the tighter the better. Around the corner, up the block, and I faced the puke-green two-family I'd come to think of as home—or at least a livable substitute--by summer's end.

I followed the news that summer with interest, but concentrated on my daily life, which between learning sign language and the basics of teaching, was challenging enough. Beyond that, I wanted to finally lose my virginity, and to prove, as my ironically-named therapist, Mrs. Love, claimed back at Northwestern, that I was simply "inexperienced" and was "perfectly capable" of having sex with women. Phil had a girlfriend back in Chicago, Greg had one in California, and I wanted a romance of my own, if only to assure myself that I was ok. Lisa was a full-figured girl from Cleveland, the niece of a family friend, who had just arrived in Oakland to attend art school. I called her up, we made a coffee date, and soon I was riding the BART (Bay Area Rapid Transit) train, going under the Bay via tunnel between San Francisco and Oakland, my time underwater an eternity. I tried not to think about what might happen in an earthquake, but was tempted to hold my breath while suspended between here and there.

Lisa had driven her purple Gremlin, American Motor's strange-looking car, its truncated rear end so ugly it was almost cute, to pick me up. I teased her about that and we seemed to connect. By our second date we were making out, both knowing this was a summer fling —she was staying out west, while I'd be heading back to Northwestern in 8 weeks. I didn't have many options for meeting women, since I was 20 and looked 15—and terribly shy around attractive women. Besides, the drinking age in California was 21 and most of the clubs wouldn't let me in. Lisa was friendly, casual, and non-threatening (plain). Soon we were talking about "doing it" at my place.

One day after work, I rode around the city on the N-Judah train trying to work up the nerve to buy a package of condoms, which were generally kept behind the pharmacy counter at local drug stores. I finally went to the counter at a store near Union Square and quietly asked for a pack of Trojans, when the middle-aged woman behind me in line said, "Imagine that, in a Rexall drugstore!" as if I'd just scored a line of cocaine. A few nights later Lisa was at my place in the Castro, where we lay together on my mattress on the floor, warding off the chill. I was nervous, unsure of exactly how it was all going to 'work,' but after ten minutes of trying, it became clear that it wasn't. I apologized, explaining that it was my first time and I had never used a condom.

Lisa was understanding and said all the right things. Eventually we had dinner, and I walked her back out to the Gremlin. We continued to date over the next month but didn't go much beyond heavy petting. On my last night in town, before I headed back to the Midwest, she came over to say goodbye. After dinner, while kissing in my bedroom, I felt a surge of interest. I'd ditched the condoms and wasn't prepared, in that moment, to have sex. But I held onto that passing sense of sexual excitement as I flew back east, still trying to prove I was something — or someone —I wasn't.

•

During my sophomore year at Northwestern, the university's administration decided to close the undergraduate School of Education, and the Deaf Education program along with it. The closure had been planned for several years, but the news was not shared with incoming students. After the decision was announced I wrote a letter to the school paper and whipped up a stream of controversy on campus. My last line, "It seems our great university has no place for teachers—ironic isn't it?" made the college look bad. Eventually they decided to allow the six sophomores in our program, including me, to graduate. But our professors began to leave, and in the middle of my junior year, so did I.

Chapter 13

Wrestling with Myself

Now I know the geographic cure doesn't work; instinctively I knew it then. But once my program at Northwestern began to crumble, I had no choice but to find another school that offered my very specialized major. So, in January 1978, I crossed over the Ohio River on Interstate 75 and passed through Kentucky and on into East Tennessee for the first time. Riding with me, a silent passenger, was my belief that I was fundamentally different, inferior to other boys and men.

During those first months at UT, I reveled in the down-home twang of my new friends, the mannered politeness of Southerners in general, and their rich heavy food—biscuits and gravy, sweet potato pie, sweet tea. I hoped to reinvent myself in Knoxville, to start over in this place so different from home, the winds coursing down from the nearby hills whispering that anything was possible.

Three decades later, back in Tennessee for the first time since the early '80s, I drove past the University of Tennessee campus on Cumberland Avenue and "the strip," a collection of low-rent bars, chain restaurants, and stores—the typical sprawl near any urban campus. Heading south, I skirted downtown Knoxville with its gold-plated Sunsphere, a leftover from the 1982 World's Fair, the last time I was in town. Then I crossed over the silt-filled Tennessee River and cruised toward South Knoxville. Turning onto Island Home Avenue, a broad boulevard with a line of oak trees in the center median, I was caught short by the gate and guardhouse that blocked the entrance to the Tennessee School for the Deaf, where I'd worked as a dorm counselor during my senior year at UT in 1979, a barrier that didn't exist during my days at the school.

I nodded to the guard and signed in, explaining that I used to live at TSD, and drove slowly along the circular drive. The "cottages," blocky, overheated brick buildings, ("firetraps," the guard called them) that formerly dotted the campus were gone, replaced with low-slung modern structures, which looked more like small houses, new and inviting. I pulled over and examined the school building and the superintendent's house that survived and stared at the vacant lot where my old cottage should have been—where there was only grass and dirt.

•

In the summer of 1978, at the end of my first semester at the University, I found a job at the Tennessee School for the Deaf. I lived in a linoleum-floored room in Cottage D, the junior-high students' dorm on the TSD campus.

At 21, I carried a knot of despair twisted in my solar plexus, the struggle to deny my sexuality. The despair kept me edgy—thinking, worrying, a labyrinth in my mind. As I went through each day, "the knot," a banding of my abdomen, appeared, muscles contracting as if to keep something from spilling out. The knot was relieved only by running, visits to the gym, or jacking off, which I did often. Meanwhile, I was still adjusting to southern life—the friendliness and the easy pace of life countered by the raw darkness of words like "nigger" and "Jew somebody down," that made me queasy and left me feeling lost, alone.

In late August, after a two-day orientation in the school's administration building, I started my split-day work schedule—6 to 8 in the morning, 3:30 to 9:30 in the evening—three days per week, and all day on weekends. On Sunday mornings, some of our kids went to church services, and I'd watch TV, a visitor in a foreign land. Cas Walker, a local legend who'd been active in Knoxville politics for generations, with a chain of grocery stores and a thick hillbilly accent, introduced talent on his weekly variety show. There I saw clogging, a form of wooden-shoe tap-dancing performed to bluegrass music, for the first time. There I heard bluegrass songs like "Rocky Top," about a small town up in the Tennessee hills where "strangers showed up lookin' for a moonshine still," with the verse, "Strangers never came back down again, reckon they never will," a half-humorous reflection of the strange country I'd been cast into. Cas Walker reminded me of my difference—of being a Northern Jew below the Mason-Dixon Line. At TSD, as a hearing man in a deaf world, I was as much an outsider as I was in the rest of Tennessee, but for different reasons.

My weekends came on Monday and Tuesday, my regular days off, when I focused on schoolwork and learning sign language. The teachers and dorm directors at the school had developed "TSD signs," traditional hand-shapes borrowed from American Sign Language and altered to accommodate English, their own versions of the SEE signs I'd learned in San Francisco. The (mostly-hearing) staff had taken ASL signs like WILL—one hand moving forward from the face, arcing out into the future—and added the initial W, to distinguish the sign from FUTURE—which had a similar motion with an F-hand. Unfortunately, TSD signs were only known and understood on campus. After graduation, deaf folks reverted to ASL.

Many of my fellow dorm counselors also attended UT. Older folks lived and worked at the school too, watching us "young ones" come and go, while they hung on year after year, embedded in the life of the school like the oaks on Island Home Avenue.

While I lived in Cottage D, surrounded by the dorm rooms of junior-high-aged deaf boys, I worked next door in 'C'—the multiply-handicapped house. My wards there possessed an array of strange behaviors; many were autistic. I learned about autism by watching Sanford, a skinny, excitable child with a round protruding belly and skin the color of dark chocolate. He'd hoot and holler, his round eyes reacting to phantoms only he could see. Danny, a short, pudgy boy with stingy brown eyes and a crooked smile, tried to get his way by biting his own arm, hitting his head against the nearest radiator, or chomping on the hand that supervised him. Many of my ten boys needed help bathing and suffered from mood swings. They had limited ability to sign and no intelligible speech. But my biggest challenge came not from the boys but from another counselor, Tim.

Tim was a lean lanky teenager, only 18 when I met him one stifling August day. A few of the other counselors, envious of his bedroom eyes and good looks, called Tim "Conway" behind his back. With his long lashes, green eyes and pompadour-high hair, he did look a bit like the country music star Conway Twitty but was much better looking, more like a '70s James Dean.

Tim favored light cotton shirts that clung to his slender, sinewy body, tendons and stringy muscles visible in his chest and arms. Those shirts, the torso underneath, and Tim's north Georgia drawl sent a frisson of excitement through me. When I heard we'd be working together, the band in my abdomen grew tighter.

To make things worse, Tim's bedroom was "Two doors down," like the Dolly Parton song popular at the time. This beautiful guy was everything I was not: cocky, strong, and a stud with women. During our first week together, we shared our stories. Tim had grown up in Rome, Georgia, ran away from home at 15, and left for good at 17. Instead of attending UT like the rest of us, he spent his free time working out, chasing women, and dreaming of becoming an airline pilot. I pictured him, looking fine, green eyes and white teeth set off against his navy blue uniform, a vision of masculine competence.

Tim teased me, laughing at my earnest efforts to please Mrs. Liston, our housemother and boss. Mrs. L was a no-nonsense Tennessean who ruled over the boys like a benevolent despot, ready to smack them whenever their offenses called for it—which, in her opinion, they often did.

I did please her. Sometimes, catching a glimpse of myself in the bathroom mirror as I directed the boys into the shower, I saw the boy/man she saw reflected in the steamy glass. An earnest-looking guy with light brown hair, liquid blue eyes and a runner's body. A face un-grooved by age but creased with worry. Someone who tried—maybe too hard—to follow orders.

Though older than Tim, I felt younger, more naive about the way life worked. Fixated, I studied him, memorizing the way he moved as if he could show me a template for manhood. After a month, Tim began to date a flashy blonde named Lena who worked in one of the girls' dorms. Lena had a Farrah Fawcett hairstyle, frost-blue eyes, and an appetite for Tim. I saw him less often.

By Thanksgiving I told my therapist, Jimmy, a doctoral student at the university, that I had "feelings" for Tim.

"So, what if you do have those feelings? Do you want to kiss him? Have you ever wanted to kiss a guy?" he asked me.

"I don't want that." While wrestling with Tim turned me on, I'd never imagined kissing him. "I can't be gay."

"You don't have enough experience to know. You're making a big deal about this guy, even though he's not an important person in your life. I think you're avoiding your anger at your parents and your feelings for women."

Hmm. That sounded reasonable. I was angry with my parents—I carried a long list of grievances. And there were girls I was drawn to, girls I liked. But I didn't fantasize about their bodies and couldn't get excited at the sight of them; it was muscular men who aroused me.

While I worried about pleasing our housemother, Tim regarded his job as a mere nuisance and a steady paycheck as he watched TV, yelling at the kids when they interfered with his favorite programs. His signs were choppy and awkward, and much slower than mine. Lips compressed in a flat line, Tim's face would redden as Sanford emitted his "Ooohhh" wail or Danny smirked and headed for the nearest radiator.

Sometimes, late in the evening—the boys bathed and fed, the TV droning on its metal stand—Tim and I would talk, or occasionally, wrestle. He'd been working on his physique, lifting dumbbells and barbells in the basement of our cottage three or four times a week. Tim wanted to show off his strength and sculpted body, and I was his nominal competition.

One day, just before Thanksgiving recess, the supervisors and dorm directors held a meeting in the living room of Cottage C. Tim and I hung out in one of the side rooms, waiting until afternoon came and we could hit the road. Our kids had already left to visit their own families, who had to take them in over school vacations, though most were none too thrilled about it.

Tim began to tease me, saying he could "whip my butt" in less than a minute. Whispering, careful not to disturb our bosses, we wrestled on one of the empty beds. Tim was strong and knew how to wrestle. My arousal strained my jeans and mixed with the shame of losing.

We left to go our separate ways—Tim to visit friends in Knoxville, me for the long drive up to Cleveland. My mind whirled. Tim didn't seem to notice my excitement, but I couldn't deny it, not on that 500-mile ride back home with only the chatter of my mind and the whine of country music radio for company.

•

As fall became winter I mastered my job. At 6:15, I led my kids into the harsh light of the dining hall, hurrying them along. I forced down the southern breakfast in the green-walled room—okra, biscuits and gravy and scrambled eggs, bathed in butter and grease. Then, marching the sleepy boys back to the dorm by 7, I nudged them to do their chores, and herded them off to school at 8.

If I didn't have an early class at UT, I'd crawl back into bed and fall into restless sleep, lulled by the hum of the air conditioner, or during winter, by the clanging steam in the ancient pipes near my bed. As the days went on, it was hard to eat, to feed a body hard-wired to desire young men. Throat closing, I took small bites and washed down the dining hall dinners—country-fried steak, meat loaf, hot dogs—with milk, ignoring the lump in my throat, which expanded daily. Somehow, I maintained my 145 pounds, the grease-laden food congealing in my stomach like a rock.

In January, Tim told me about a dream he'd had the previous night. In the dream, he wrestled with another counselor at our school, and I was there, too—watching, hiding in a locker. I flushed, my heart racing as I listened. The other counselor—a gruff balding hard of hearing man—couldn't be of interest to Tim. What was he trying to tell me? Had he uncovered my secret on a subconscious level? I didn't have the nerve to ask. I laughed off the dream instead, pretending not to care.

A few weeks later, a counselor left the junior high boys' dorm, and Mrs. Gilmore, the gray-haired no-nonsense housemother—tougher even than Mrs. Liston—needed a replacement. I applied for the job, and soon began my new position, supervising 32 hyperactive deaf boys. Now I had a new challenge, trying to decipher the rapid-fire sign language of those teenagers. I struggled to keep up, to capture the rhythm of each boy's signs. There was little Adam, the son of deaf parents, who signed with lightning speed and fingerspelled even faster, while I gamely tried to catch his meaning. There was Jim, a thin, laconic, brown-faced boy, who signed slowly, in a laid-back southern style that was reflected in everything he did. And there were others, who couldn't spell, and who hadn't really mastered English. Gradually I picked up more of the language—their language—but I was constantly reminded of my difference, of being hearing in a deaf world.

While I learned a form of sign language from my boys, I tried to help them master written English—a sore point for many. I began an extra credit reading program, searching the Knoxville Public Library for "high interest/low vocabulary" books on sports heroes like Willie Mays and Joe Namath. A bar chart tracked the winners, who had to answer a few basic questions to get credit for each volume. Those who read the most books earned a reward—a trip to Dairy Queen. Soon I had a small group of avid readers, or page-turners, determined to collect their prize.

Though Tim still lived two doors down, I saw him less often. Sometimes, I stopped by his room at night—on those rare occasions when he wasn't balling Lena—and he told me stories of other young women he'd conquered. Wracked with jealousy of his prowess and the feelings I wouldn't name, I'd slink off to my room. Meanwhile, I pictured the two of us wrestling, him pinning me again with a cocky smile as I drifted off to sleep.

•

Now, staring at the ground where the old cottages should have been, a middle-aged man no longer afraid of his desire for men, I recalled the way Tim at 18 radiated a 'Nothing's gonna happen to me, I'm gonna live forever' confidence I never had. Looking back, I wondered how much of that cockiness was false bravado, his need to preen like a rooster in a barnyard a cover for his own shaky sexuality. It was only in hindsight, looking through the clarity of my rear view mirror, when I sensed that Tim's fear of not knowing where he might end up, and of whom he might love, was similar to my own.

Chapter 14

Reverberations

In the early 1930s, A.G. Bell, Cleveland's school for deaf children, was located on East 55th Street, on the city's east side. My mother recalled my grandmother taking Jerry there as a young boy, down Superior Avenue via streetcar several times a week for speech training.

I conjure my grandmother as a young woman, her beauty starting to fade. On a late winter day in 1934, twenty-nine-year-old Fay Cohen led her three-year-old son Jerry down the steps of their two-family house on Saywell Road in East Cleveland and around the corner onto East 123rd Street, where they'd catch the streetcar and ride west toward downtown.

As a younger woman, Fay Weinbaum modeled for a local furrier. Now, during the dark days of the Depression, she wore a wool coat, broken in and frayed. Her son, this boy who couldn't hear her voice or speak her name, walked beside her, holding her hand.

It was hard not to notice the sadness in Ben's eyes when he looked at Jerry, a pain they didn't talk about. The drug store drained his energy and left him quiet. Fay felt Ben's disappointment when he looked at her, too, as if she'd failed him, as if the whole thing was her fault. Maybe it was. One of the doctors suggested that a fall in the seventh month of her pregnancy might have damaged Jerry's auditory nerve. The doctors didn't know why Jerry was deaf, but they were certain of his prognosis—no cure, no treatment. Their son would always live in a world of silence, of lipreading and artificial speech.

Fay pulled the boy along, his tiny mitten-covered hands fitting neatly in her smooth palms. He liked the streetcar, the excursions into the city, and by now, a full year after they began these journeys, he knew what to do. She didn't have to explain everything, a useless task anyway.

The wind, whipping off Lake Erie, ripped through her sensible coat. Jerry's face, with its dark eyes and olive complexion, contrasted with her pale beauty, which reddened in the March cold. She'd outfitted Jerry in rough wool pants, a miniature copy of his father's, along with a shirt two-sizes too large, a puffy blue coat, scarf and mittens.

The streetcar lurched up and disgorged a few passengers. Jerry stood and waited, his eyes wide.

What was the silent movie in his mind? Did it have a soundtrack—not music, but rhythm? Was it dead quiet, as if he lived underwater?

Fay tugged Jerry along and helped him take big boy steps into the car, which smelled of men, tobacco, hair oil, and coal. The black sheen of his Buster Browns reflected the morning light.

A scene emerges. My grandmother uses the feminine wiles from her brief modeling career. She smiles, the way she'd been taught at I.J. Fox, the way she'd done for those newspaper ads. A businessman in a pinstriped suit, about 35, his thinning black hair parted neatly to one side, springs up and motions her to a seat near the coal stove, tipping his hat. Nodding thanks in response to his yellow smile—he must be a heavy smoker, like Ben—she settles in, warning Jerry to stay on her right, away from the black heat.

The streetcar, black and gray and stiflingly hot, makes a gradual turn onto Superior Avenue, one of Cleveland's grand streets, with its tall elms and formerly great homes settling into disuse. As the streetcar rocks side to side, Jerry squirms beneath Fay's protective arm. She watches him, mouthing "calm down," tapping his chest and smiling. Looking up at her, he's a blank slate. She watches herself being recorded in his brown eyes and wonders again what he's thinking.

The car sways slowly toward Public Square and the city center, stopping and starting in jerky rhythm. Too soon, long before her energy is restored, they reach the intersection of Superior and East 55th Street. Five minutes later they're standing in front of A.G. Bell School.

At the school, Jerry is prodded and poked by adults who hold their faces too close to his. Touching his chin, they move his lips to mimic theirs; he becomes a hand puppet, soft and pliable. Fay sits nearby, patting him, mouthing 'pay attention' and 'watch her mouth,' in her ineffectual way. On previous visits, he'd learned to say his name—Jehree—the two syllables skittering around in his throat like marbles.

He learns to say Mama and Daddy, over and over, so that Fay can make out the words. On each visit, he copies the silent lips of a grayhaired speech teacher who tells him, "You will learn to talk," mouthing the words and pointing to her thin lips, the same mantra every week, until he can finally understand her.

On the way home, exhausted, Jerry closes his eyes, shutting out the visual noise known only to deaf children who watch everything and hear nothing. Both of them, mother and son, doze in the car until the conductor calls out, "123rd," and Fay jolts the boy awake.

Over the next several years, my grandmother would lose much of her own hearing. Though a specialist performed surgery the calcification or bone quickly grew back, and my grandmother turned into the woman I knew so many years later, who spoke in a quavery voice and wore two hearing aids.

From A.G. Bell, Jerry went on to Superior School in East Cleveland and then to Kirk Junior High School, schools with special oral programs for deaf children. Hundreds, if not thousands of hours were spent fulfilling Alexander Graham Bell's dictum that all deaf children must learn to speak. Eventually, by the time Jerry reached junior high, he did develop (partially) intelligible speech. But my uncle, with his lifeless auditory nerve, could never speak like a hearing person.

How much of his spirit died during all those years of trying to follow the instructions of his oral-method teachers, of being told what to do by his parents and doctors, as if he couldn't think for himself?

Yes, Jerry learned to speak but, as his daughter said years later, "at what cost?"

•

One morning in January 1980 I walked into A.G. Bell School on Woodland Avenue in Cleveland, looking for work as a substitute teacher. (The school had moved to a new building on the eastern edge of the city around 1970). I'd come home after five years of college. After graduation, I was planning to spend six months traveling around Europe with my brother Alex. But I'd developed a fear of flying to go along with my fear of everything else: losing weight, getting depressed, sex with women, potential sex with men, and was looking for an excuse not to go on the trip.

When I arrived back in Knoxville in December 1979 after student teaching in Vermont, I met Jimmy, my therapist, a few days before graduation. A solidly-built graduate student with thick red hair and a matching beard, he reminded me of a Viking by way of Oklahoma City. We met in a coffee shop off campus. I told him I was worn out from student teaching and not sure if I wanted to go on the trip. Jimmy appraised me with his hazel eyes across the Formica table. "I don't usually give advice, but when are you gonna stop running away and deal with your life?" When one of my best friends followed that up by saying, "Why don't you just come home?" I decided to scrap the trip and return to Cleveland.

Six weeks later, I nervously walked into the boxy-looking school—the worst of late 1960s architecture with its stingy slotted windows—and went straight to the main office. The principal, a blonde-haired woman of about 35, introduced herself, showed me into her office, and examined my resume. She smiled, pleased to see someone with a degree in deaf education literally walk in off the street. I seemed to be qualified—she couldn't really tell—since she didn't know sign language. I learned that she had recently taken over the principal's position at A.G. Bell, along with the directorship of the Sunbeam School for physically handicapped children across the street. But she had no experience teaching deaf children and couldn't communicate with the students under her care.

The administration and teachers of the Cleveland Public Schools had been locked in an ongoing war over wages and benefits. Teachers had gone on strike for the first eleven weeks of the school year and would be making those days up well into the summer of 1980. Hard feelings remained, and tainted the atmosphere of the school. During the strike, one of the second grade teachers had decamped to New Zealand with her Kiwi husband, and now the principal needed someone to replace her.

Twenty minutes later, I was offered a full-time job. Instead of skimming by as a substitute, I'd earn a salary of $10,800 per year and benefits. I'd be a "Total Communication" teacher, using a combination of sign language and spoken English in a school named for Alexander Graham Bell, the father of the oral approach to deaf education. Bell had a deaf mother and a deaf wife—he married one of his former students—and believed deafness could be virtually eliminated by discouraging intermarriage among deaf people. He moved to outlaw sign language in the schools, removed deaf teachers, and vowed to eliminate deaf culture. In Bell's view, the deaf had no choice but to assimilate into the hearing world.

I knew that Mr. Bell would have been furious at the changes taking place at 'his' school. They had recently converted from a strictly oral approach, in which students were forbidden to use sign language, to one that allowed both oral and signing classes. The teachers practiced a strange variety of methods. Some didn't sign at all, while others signed a little but weren't fluent. Several of the younger teachers, like me, used some form of sign language with their students. Very few of the boys and girls at A.G. Bell had intelligible speech—and those that did were usually hard of hearing, not deaf. By the time they reached junior high, most of the students relied on sign language to communicate.

After my interview, I began teaching a class of six second-grade girls. I didn't force them to talk; none of my students had intelligible speech despite years of training. Instead I focused on giving them language by signing and using my voice. During that first year I learned by trial and error, with very little guidance from A.G. Bell's master teacher, who didn't sign and had nothing to offer me.

The next year I moved to Columbus, hoping that a new setting away from childhood memories I preferred to forget would make my life easier. I found an apartment on the city's north side and a therapist and began working to strengthen my attraction to the opposite sex, to change myself. For the next several years, while teaching at the Ohio School for the Deaf, I dated women, saw my therapist, and suppressed my longing for men.

•

Over time, I discovered that moving 150 miles from Cleveland didn't change anything. I could no more become straight than my uncle could learn to hear.

Chapter 15

Getting Out

By the mid-1980s and my fifth and last year at the Ohio School for the Deaf, my thoughts were of getting out: out of teaching, out of the deaf school, and out of the closet.

During my initial years at OSD, while I sporadically dated women and followed the news stories of the "gay cancer" that had appeared in San Francisco and New York City, I tried to concentrate on teaching. I longed to bring my deaf charges into a new world of learning, to inspire them. But my students, 15 and 16-year-olds, many of whom couldn't read or write, were unmoved by my determination.

The teacher in the next room, Marilyn, seemed to have all the answers. Organized to a fault, workbooks stacked in neat rows, assignments calibrated for each student, her classroom hummed like a well-oiled machine. She'd been teaching at OSD for four years but it might have been forty. Hungry for lesson plans, worksheets and new ideas, I wore a path to Marilyn's door, picking up useful tips that didn't ease my sense of inadequacy. Marilyn couldn't have been so competent her first year, I told myself hopefully. And she put in countless hours of prep time at home, after school. How could I match her level of dedication? Did I even want to?

Instead I yelled, muttered, pleaded. Gesturing roughly in ASL, raising my voice in English, I'd eventually revert to, "Shut up!" and occasionally, "Get the hell out of my room!" Kenny Poole, a pinkish-skinned boy with freckles and a shock of white hair above blue-gray eyes, was one of my more difficult students. A frustrated 16-year-old with a condition called Waardenburg's Syndrome, Kenny had a touch of mental retardation, a third-grade reading level, and enough sense to know that his twin sister back home in small-town Lima—beautiful, hearing, "normal," had none of his disabilities. Kenny was prone to tantrums, turning over desks and threatening to punch me as his pale face turned crimson.

Eventually, I learned to teach kids like Kenny and to even enjoy some of them. Each had their own foibles, sense of humor, quirks. Two years after our initial confrontations, I worked with Kenny again. In the interim, he'd matured and grown more comfortable in his own skin.

In his junior year, Kenny began working at McDonald's, earning minimum wage through the school's work-study program. Looking resplendent in his blue uniform and white cap, he'd head off to work from my classroom each afternoon, his face glistening with pride when I asked him, jokingly, "for a small loan." Each morning, before work, we'd review English vocabulary and basic math—figuring out how much money he'd take home each week. We made sense of a bus schedule, an application for a Social Security card, a city map.

The next year I had Kenny again, as a senior. (He was the first and last student I taught for three years). By then, we'd become friends. He mimicked the way I signed, with my hearing "accent." I'd tease him, gently, when he became frustrated with a math problem, scrunching up my face like a prune. My forehead creased with mock worry, I mirrored the way Kenny's brow furrowed under his white hair. Eventually, he'd smile and laugh, his chipped front tooth jutting over his lower lip. Later, during spring of Kenny's senior year, I agreed to be a chaperone for the OSD prom.

In a photo I'd taken just before we all boarded the OSD bus before dinner, Kenny stood in front of an old beige Duesenberg coupe, elbow resting on the passenger door, left foot on the running board. Several antique cars were displayed on campus, part of the seniors' graduation celebration. Kenny wore a powder blue tux with a matching bow tie, a hint of a smile visible below his pale mustache, the color of corn stalks. Kenny didn't have a date, but many of my "kids" were going solo. That night, after dinner at Max and Erma's, a local chain restaurant, and roller-skating, we were off to a special midnight showing of "Terms of Endearment" complete with subtitles for the deaf.

Bleary at 2 am, we stumbled off the bus back at OSD. In a few hours I'd be back at school, bracing for another day. Kenny wouldn't be there; he had officially graduated. The next morning, I actually missed him.

•

My college courses had prepared me, in a cursory way, to teach normal deaf children. After graduation, the State of Ohio certified me to instruct deaf and hard-of-hearing children from kindergarten through high school, as if knowing a bit about deafness and having a degree in special education made me an expert in all subjects. But I knew little about teaching math, science, or of how to work with multiply-handicapped children. The real students, the flesh and blood kids who filled my small classes and challenged me daily at OSD after I'd moved to Columbus in the fall of 1981, were not simply deaf. OSD was a residential school, (students returned home once or twice a month on weekends and for summer vacation), located on the north side of Columbus, its large fenced-in campus surrounded by middle-class homes. The city itself was an unremarkable test-market town, Middle American in its blandness. Locked into the flat Central Ohio landscape, surrounded by cornfields, life revolved around Ohio State University and the fate of its football Buckeyes, state government, and shopping at Eastland, Westland and Northland malls. But Columbus, unlike Cleveland, was growing steadily and full of twenty-somethings like me, and I wanted space to create a life in a new city where I had no history.

OSD was better equipped than any other school in the state to serve deaf children. Most of the teachers were fluent in American Sign Language; several were deaf themselves. The school was supported by the State of Ohio, and all deaf children over the age of three were eligible for admission. But hearing parents were often reluctant to send their young children to a residential school hours away from home. Many of the students came later, as teenagers. By then they had lost precious time, attending public schools with no programs for the deaf, or poorly-organized ones, sitting in classes with teachers who could not sign, deprived of any language—English or ASL.

At OSD deaf children met others like themselves, and saw deaf adults as teachers, and house-parents in the dorms; they had deaf role models. Arriving at our school, most of the latecomers quickly learned sign language, but few became fluent in reading or writing English; the primary years for language development lost, wasted.

Some students did succeed academically. Every year, the best went on to two and four-year colleges, including Gallaudet University, the liberal arts college for the deaf in Washington, D.C., and the National Technical Institute for the Deaf in Rochester, New York. Unfortunately, I didn't teach those children.

Since I had no seniority, I was offered a job in the school's Work Study Program. There, I taught independent living skills to the school's "academic failures." Most of my students couldn't read beyond primary school level, fill out a job application, or write a clear English sentence. Over the next five years, I worked with a stream of children, some with autism, mental retardation, and/or cerebral palsy, and others who were simply deaf, and who had languished in their local schools.

During my first years in Columbus, I had weekly therapy sessions in a small home office a few miles from the deaf school. My therapist, Deborah, was a plain woman of about 40, simple and direct, with black glasses and an exotic accent I couldn't place. Later I learned she'd grown up in England and Israel, and carried a mix of both—the no-nonsense truth telling of an Israeli leavened with the politeness of an Englishwoman. In an early session, when I confessed my attraction for men, Deborah claimed I was simply inexperienced.

"You haven't had much experience with women," she said, offering her certainty as an antidote for my doubt. Shifting in her chair, Deborah smiled and rearranged her sensible gray wool skirt. If only I could arrange my attractions so easily.

"Your sexuality doesn't have to be such an issue. If you want to have sex with women, have sex with women." She shrugged, the universal Jewish symbol for 'It's no big deal.'

"Besides, if I saw you walking down the street, I wouldn't think you were gay," she said.

Deborah was a disciple of Albert Ellis, a well-known psychologist and prolific author who believed that homosexuality was pathology, a condition that could be cured with the right attitude. I spent my years with Deborah reading books about Rational Emotive Therapy, and trying to follow its edicts. RET claimed that people think their way in and out of emotional states; they create their realities through self-talk and beliefs. His books had titles like, "How to Cope with a Fatal Illness" and "A New Guide to Rational Living."

According to Ellis and Deborah, I could overcome my lifelong depression and anxiety by practicing rational thinking, and shift my sexual attraction from men to women. But no matter how hard I tried, I couldn't banish the thoughts of muscular men from my fantasies and dreams, or cast off my constant depression.

Finally, in June 1985, after ten years of on-again, off-again therapy, I began to creep out of the closet. Much of that therapy, including the past four years with Deborah, had focused on how to achieve the Olympian victory of a good fuck, thereby proving my manhood. I believed that if I could get that rite of passage down pat, I'd be fit to join my male companions in the real world. But I never did succeed; with women, I was a bust in bed.

Eventually I surrendered. One Memorial Day weekend, I admitted I was powerless over the hard-wired impulses of my body and the fantasies of my mind. On that Friday, the teachers were summoned to a meeting in the OSD library. There, our superintendent announced that for the first time in forty years, several of us would be laid off, based on seniority.

There went my job, and my plans for the fall. The next day, I went to my local bookstore and bought a copy of "What Color Is Your Parachute?" a career planning and job hunter's guide. But as I began to read the colorful paperback book, it became agonizingly clear that I couldn't find a new career until I'd dealt with the desires roiling my mind and body.

A few days later, I walked into Deborah's office and announced, "I think I'm gay and I need to find out for sure." And so my therapist told me of an old friend who had recently come out to her. Don, a recovering alcoholic in his fifties, had denied his sexuality for many years, using work and drink to suppress his desire for men. Now, after decades of misery, he was finally coming out. He attended a weekly gay men's group for Catholics that met at the Paulist Center at Ohio State. I went to his house, heard his story and his warning, "Don't waste your life like I did." When Don invited me to attend a group session, I explained that I was Jewish. He shrugged and told me to come anyway.

And so I did. One evening that June, propelled by my visceral need to meet other gay men, I walked into the Paulist Center, an unremarkable brick building on Lane Avenue across from the OSU campus, which served as the Catholic student union at the university. I entered the dark edifice with its royal blue carpeting and its unfamiliar smells, which hinted at strange Christian rites I'd never witnessed.

The program focused on how to protect oneself from AIDS. Petrified of both the specter of the disease and the gay men who filled the small chapel, I watched and listened carefully. The speaker, an earnest young man from the Stonewall Union, an advocacy group named for the Stonewall Bar in New York City where the gay liberation movement began in the late 1960s, passed out handouts warning of the dangers of the virus. In the mid-'80s, many questions about transmission still remained; kissing was considered safe, but deep kissing was in the "less safe" category. Other strange activities like "rimming" and "fisting" were considered unsafe, as was unprotected anal sex.

The conversation, the room full of men, and the talk of AIDS buzzed through me, electric. I'd never made love to another man, never even kissed one. Which of these activities would I like? How could I avoid AIDS and still have a sex life?

The meeting passed quickly, the two hours a glimpse of possibility, of coming out of isolation. Could I find a connection with these men, some of who seemed just like me?

At OSD, my struggles continued. The layoffs were rescinded, but I found the work tedious and exhausting. The year before, I'd taught a lanky boy named Corey, with huge hands and feet and a dead-eyed stare that haunted me. Seventeen-years-old and almost six feet tall, with stringy muscles and restless energy, Corey had been in and out of 50 foster homes and at least one psychiatric hospital. Six months earlier, he'd been suspended from OSD for slipping his medication into my friend Marilyn's soda and "trying to kill her," knowing that his psychiatric medication could make her ill, at least.

The juvenile court judges didn't know what to do with a recalcitrant deaf boy. On his visits to court, Corey was a master actor, expressing deep remorse when he felt none, and pledging never to misbehave again. After his most recent assault, the judge fined him $50 and sent him back to the deaf school, straight into my classroom. Thankfully, the other children in my class usually followed my directions. Cal, a hyperactive, beanpole-thin boy who signed, walked and thought with house-on-fire urgency, helped keep Corey in check, threatening him with bodily harm if he stepped out of line, and literally watching my back.

Finally, near the end of the school year, the school psychologist and I got Corey evaluated at the Central Ohio Psychiatric Hospital, our local state facility. Hoping that I could spare another teacher the stress I'd endured for the past nine months, I met with a staff psychiatrist at COPH. The doctor explained that while Corey had some "socialization issues," he wasn't mentally ill according to the medical definition of the term, and was ineligible for admission. When I complained that Corey had threatened to kill me and had expressed no remorse for punching, kicking and threatening other students, the doctor shrugged; there was nothing he could do. I'd recently learned that several years earlier, while he was a resident at this same hospital, Corey had sprayed an orderly with lighter fluid and set the poor man on fire. They were not anxious to take him back.

After surviving Corey, and when I was recalled from my threatened layoff, I discovered I would be teaching the group we teachers called "the lowest of the low."Those children were high school seniors in name only; by state law they would graduate the next spring, at the age of 21. But unlike my other students, who could get entry-level jobs doing maintenance or working in fast-food restaurants, the "low-low group" was destined for sheltered workshops and group homes. So by the fall of 1985, I knew my days at OSD were numbered.

•

A few weeks after my visit to the Paulist Center, I traveled to New Zealand alone, and then continued on to Australia with an old friend from college. Meanwhile, the news of Rock Hudson's AIDS-related decay and his desperate trip to Paris for an experimental medication blared from Australian television. Even in Perth, 10,000 miles from home on the shores of the Indian Ocean, I couldn't escape Hudson's demise and its implications for my own life. Now that I'd finally found the nerve to begin coming out, I was shadowed by a death sentence. It seemed that sex with another man = death.

I returned to Columbus at the end of summer isolated and tired of being alone. Since there was no Jewish gay men's group in Columbus, I returned to the Catholic one. (I learned later that the Paulists were "progressives" in the Church, and that the local bishop had OK'd the group's meetings, as long as the leaders promised not to "promote" the gay lifestyle). On this September night, the Paulist Center still whispered of the strange rituals of the Catholic Church. As I entered, the air felt cool against my skin, sweat pooling against my polo shirt.

I pasted a smile onto my face and slipped into the chapel. Small groups of men clumped together, chatting and drifting toward a circle of chairs. A wooden crucifix dominated the brick wall across from my seat. Father Charlie, an older priest in his sixties, who considered himself gay but practiced celibacy, and another younger priest in his thirties conferred, preparing for the meeting. I sat down and an impulse to stand and run seized me. Instead, I forced myself to remain seated, shifting my weight on the hard wood.

We began with an icebreaker—who are we, and why did we come to the group? Paired with a mustachioed man with dark brown eyes and a deep voice, my story spilled out. Larry listened, nodded, and threw in supportive comments. "I'm just coming out, I explained, don't know any gay men, and just happen to be Jewish." Larry's eyes remained heavy, his face relaxed in a smile. The icebreaker ended and my new friend introduced me to the group.

Larry helped me come out as a Jew, and to my relief no one called out, "You killed Jesus!" or looked upset because I was there. I'd found a place to call home, at least on Tuesday nights.

My social life was limited by my insecurities and a lack of style. Tall and thin, I wore tortoise-shell glasses too big for my face, while my scraggly beard would have shamed a goat. My pale face, with its blond eyebrows, red-blond mustache and red beard, was a mélange of colors that contrasted with my old corduroys and wrinkled shirts. A thick gold chain, which I'd worn for many years, completed the fashion disaster.

Still, a hunky younger man named Carl noticed me. Carl was slim and muscular, with hazel eyes and olive skin. In November, after I'd become a Tuesday night men's group regular, Carl invited me to go out with him and his boyfriend to a local new-wave gay bar. Since his "friend" was also in the group, I'd kept Carl at a distance. But after my long years of pining for men while dating women, my resolve began to weaken. And when he fixed me with a soulful stare, I couldn't say no.

•

There were eight students in my class during my last year at the deaf school, each difficult in their own way. Vance drooled and babbled, a stream that was impossible to understand, interspersed with an inquisitive "How're you?" about thirty times a day. Rusty was autistic, and drew pictures of buxom women he called "big girls," while ignoring his flesh-and-blood classmates. But my toughest student was Billy. A short stocky boy with autism and mental retardation, Billy possessed an innate talent for annoying his instructors; he was an idiot savant in teacher harassment.

One December afternoon, I listed 20 vocabulary words on the blackboard. I gave my students a pile of magazines and asked them to find pictures for each of the words: chicken, fish, horse, and other animals. Billy cut out a picture of a horse—tall, black, majestic—and labeled it "chicken," drawing out the word in lumpy childlike letters. I corrected him and saw the flat line of his mouth curve upward in a sadistic smile.

"No," I signed, "horse." Billy's brown eyes, which often looked empty, as if no one were home, grew dark, opaque.

"Chicken," he replied, forming the beak-like sign near his mouth. I sighed, shook my head, and grabbed the picture from his hands.

The game was on—Billy, at 5'2", trying to pull my arm down and snatch the picture as his mantra continued, "chicken, chicken," and me, at 6'1," refusing to hand it over. Clearly this was the highlight of his day. Finally, I yanked my arm from his grasp, balled up the picture and threw it out a nearby window. A minute later, Billy was outside that same window, standing in the rain. Leaning into my classroom, smiling his cockeyed smile, his pudgy thumb and finger came together and signed, "chicken."

I motioned him back inside, and quickly locked my classroom door. Light but insistent tapping continued for 10 minutes, until Marilyn called out from the room next door, "Is there a problem over there?"

Mildly embarrassed, I let Billy back into my classroom, where he promptly smoothed out his crumpled wet horse, taped it down onto his writing paper, and wrote "chicken."

•

Thanksgiving weekend, 1985: After two days back home in Cleveland, I sped back to Columbus and prepared myself for my first visit to a gay bar. What should I wear? How would I fend off the come-ons from hot, horny men with tight jeans and big muscles? I'd be meeting Carl and his boyfriend Andrew at the Garage, the popular dance bar downtown. I tried blue jeans, corduroys, shirts tight and loose, but nothing worked.

Jerry and Fay- 1931   Jerry and Rita- 1932

Jerry (upper right) with Papa Ben, Nanna Fay and other relatives- 1950

Jerry and Doug- 1953

Jerry on his first wedding day- 1958

Jerry and second wife- 1974

The author as a skeleton-1960

Alex, Dad, Mom and me, mid-70s

Me at 2 years- 1959

On vacation- 1968

Ready for prom- 1974

The young teacher- 1981

A new storyteller- 2000

Reading at a local
bookstore, about 2007

Facing middle age- 2005

A few hours later, decked out in jeans and a black T-shirt, I followed my friends into a cave-like room, with black walls surrounding the dance floor. The thumping dance music, and the electric energy of Soft Cell's "Tainted Love" pulsated in my chest. Shadows in the darkness moved in time with the music. A disco ball threw silver shards onto those dark walls. After a few minutes I left my new friends and found the men's room. I walked in as a tall, good-looking Asian woman primped before the mirror. She was beautiful, with cinnamon-colored skin and almond eyes. I tried not to stare, did my business, and returned to Carl.

As the woman walked by, I told Carl I'd seen her in the men's restroom. He laughed; "she" was a man in drag. While I knew that some gay or "trans" men dressed up in women's clothes, I was amazed by her sultry femininity, the illusion 'she' conveyed so well. But my attention quickly went back to Carl, the tightness of his body, and the way his shirt clung to his toned chest.

Then we all headed toward the dance floor. Initially I felt awkward as the other men swiveled and rocked in their skin-tight jeans. I'd always been a confident dancer, but gay men had a different rhythm, the music slithering through their collective groins like a snake. Carl called me the next day and the one after that to flirt, to talk about the group, to complain that his boyfriend didn't understand him. According to Carl, they weren't committed, but Andrew felt differently. I didn't want to become the "other woman" in a domestic dispute, a home-wrecker. Finally, Carl asked me out.

I hemmed and hawed, torn by guilt and curiosity.

"It's only dinner," he said.

A raw day in early December, and my throat ached. I'd spent seventh period chasing two of my students across OSD's sprawling campus. After lunch, Jimmy, a more able student, decided to tease Billy. Billy responded by pinching Jimmy in the groin—hard. Soon the race was on, as Jimmy took off from the campus greenhouse, where I'd been teaching my kids to plant seeds, followed by Billy, intent on squeezing Jimmy's private parts once more. Off they ran—Jimmy tall, lean and scared, Billy short, blocky and determined, and me—followed by the rest of my class. I had a sore throat, a rotten cold, and a nasty disposition.

Billy was intercepted by another teacher and handed over to the "Crisis Intervention Team," a group of teachers trained in the fine art of restraint. One of the team members had heard the ruckus, and they coalesced like a SWAT team. By the time I reached my classroom, Billy was on his way out, two of the larger male teachers lugging him toward the principal's office. Meanwhile, I calmed Jim down and sent the others on their way.

Back home, I picked up the phone to cancel my evening with Carl—my first date with a man—ready to blame my sore throat. Then I stopped, took a breath, and put the phone down.

We went to the Venetian, a casual Italian restaurant near Ohio State. The campus hangout, with its red-checked tablecloths, soft lighting, and cheap food, never failed to lighten my mood. As the warm pasta and dark beer settled in my stomach I began to relax. During dinner, I amused Carl with tales of life at the deaf school, his hazel eyes focused only on me. As I drove my Datsun Pulsar back toward home, Carl took my right hand, tracing circles in my palm.

Sitting on my $100 plaid couch—the first new piece of furniture I'd ever owned—Carl stroked my thigh. "We don't have to do anything you don't want to do—we'll take it slow." Taking my chin in one hand, he kissed my lips, softly at first, then harder. Then he sucked my tongue, his eyes searching, urgent. I closed my eyes and tasted him—a mix of salt and stubble, my first kiss with a man. Tickling my neck, he stroked me lightly, carefully. Sometime later, I led the way upstairs to the mattress on the floor of my shag-carpeted bedroom.

On that bed I understood for the first time in my 28 years that a kiss between two men, a warm embrace, wasn't wrong. Making love wasn't about gender, but simply the attraction between two people.

We stayed on my mattress until 3 o'clock the next afternoon, kissing, staring, and dozing off. That morning I called in sick without guilt. After all, I knew my students would be there waiting for me, in the days, weeks, and months to come, until they graduated the following June, and until I left the deaf school for the next phase of my life in Boston.

●

A month after my date with Carl, I decided to 'come out' to my father. Over the previous eight years Dad and I had bonded, one man to another. It began with a letter I sent him from Knoxville on my 21st birthday, when I explained that I knew of his affair, (which had ended years earlier), was angry about his extramarital activities and their effect on our family, and loved him anyway. After sending the letter I literally held my breath, wondering if he would fly into a rage—the way he sometimes did when I broke the rules as a boy—and disown me as I faced my senior year in college. (My parents were paying for my college education). But after receiving the letter my father called me up and told me that he loved me and appreciated my honesty. That led to more conversations and more connection—I began hugging him when I was 25, and soon my father was embracing my brothers and I on a regular basis—so that by the winter of 1986 I could talk to my father about almost anything; he'd become a guide imbued with a patience in short supply in my youth.

Still, I wondered how to broach the subject of my sexuality. In the 1980s most people associated gay men with AIDS, promiscuity, and the closet. Though my father had become more open-minded after his heart attack, I had no idea how my sexual orientation would affect our relationship. He lived in a world populated by engineers and businessmen and had voted for Ronald Reagan. I had several friends who had been cast out of their families. Would I be next?

It seemed unlikely. I'd already come out to my mother, and while she wasn't overjoyed at the news, she handled it calmly. After that fateful May weekend when I was temporarily laid off from OSD, I told Mom about my long-held fear of my sexual orientation. "If you're gay, you're gay," she said, surprising me with her matter-of-fact tone. I asked her not to tell my father, and to give me time to come to terms with it myself.

Now, half a year later, I didn't want to tell my Dad in person (too loaded) or by phone (too awkward). Instead, I decided to write him another letter. The letter was short, simple, to the point—I had struggled with my sexuality for many years, was finally accepting my orientation—something that was a basic part of my nature--and hoped he would, too.

It was a Wednesday in January and I was in my classroom at OSD, trying, without much luck, to concentrate on the morning's lesson. I'd mailed the letter the day before and now my heart was skipping beats as I realized my father would receive the news within a day, and that once my secret was out our relationship would be changed forever.

Now that my father was an integral part of my life, I didn't want to lose him. At 10:30 am I had a one-hour planning period; I did the mental math and figured I could run back to my apartment and call Mom, who might reassure me that Dad wouldn't freak out and reject me. As it happened, my father was home that day, too; since his heart attack in the early '70s he often took Wednesdays off. Evidently he overheard my mother's reassuring words, and after a few minutes he got on the phone and said, "I heard part of your conversation, and I just want you to know I love and respect you, and this doesn't change anything."

I cried then, and again after I hung up the phone, relief flooding my body. That night my father called me at home, (he had received my letter) repeated that he loved me, and said that I would always be his son. A few years later, after he died of a second heart attack at 61, I found my coming out letter under "mementos" in a neatly labeled file my father kept in his basement workshop. Shortly after his death my mother told me that Dad was initially surprised by my revelation, and when he hung up the phone with me on that January day in 1986, he wept, too. But after a few months, he 'got' that I hadn't changed—I was still fundamentally the son he knew and loved. Ultimately, my revelation brought us closer, an intimacy I cherished for those two brief years before his death.

Chapter 16

Taking up Space

One day near the end of my first residency at Kripalu, the yoga center where I lived in the early 1990s, I went for a walk with my friend Gary. We'd worked together for the past two months as Kitchen Support Staff, or as we called it—Karmic Seva Slaves—one department of the large Kripalu kitchen, responsible for feeding 700 residents and guests three times a day. ("Seva" was the name for each department in the ashram, and for the act of working selflessly as a form of personal growth and service to the guru.) Those three months had been a crucible for me; I didn't learn much about cooking but I gained great insight into my need for connection and community, and of how I reacted when I came up against the emotional waves of my own fear.

The intervening five years in Boston had led me to a graduate degree in higher education administration, a job as a career counselor at Boston University, and a life in which I'd become increasingly comfortable as an 'out' gay man (though I remained mostly closeted at BU). I liked my work, particularly when it morphed into teaching career-related courses for undergraduates in the University's business school. And yet I gave it all up to live at Kripalu, a decision that alarmed my family and led me to question whether I was running away from my life or delving more deeply into it.

The truth was that despite the externals—a good job, a comfortable apartment and a small network of friends—I remained fundamentally alone. Depressed, anxious, I still carried 'the knot' in my solar plexus, a remnant of my college years and my sense that life was turbulent, a series of small updrafts and steep downdrafts, a white-knuckled flight I simply tried to survive.

Kripalu was well-designed to stoke those fears and to make its residents—especially short-term ones like me, who signed up for the "Spiritual Lifestyle Training" program—uncomfortable. Unlike the long-term group who had lived at the ashram for a decade or more, we were still adjusting to the strange culture, the "Reform Hinduism" of the guru and his followers, were still used to the pace of a life outside the proscribed routines of life within the ashram walls.

I'd gone to Kripalu, not out of a quest for spiritual fulfillment, but for healing. (I've since discovered the two are not unrelated). I was chronically tense, obsessed by fears ranging from premature death—I was convinced I would suffer an early heart attack like my father—to my conviction I was unworthy of love and destined to be alone.

All my fears and vulnerabilities were exposed during those first weeks at the ashram. I knew that gay men and lesbians lived there and were accepted as individuals, but the Center's policies reflected the guru's discomfort and the senior administration's ignorance of gay people and their needs. Kripalu was divided along gender lines—men lived with men/women with women, and some workplaces were divided in similar ways, though most departments had been "integrated" by the time I arrived. All non-married men and women were supposed to practice bramacharya, which was described as "moderation in all things," but which meant celibacy outside of marriage. Same-sex marriage was not offered as an option, so most gay residents left after a few years.

Casual conversations between members of the opposite sex outside of the workplace were still discouraged. During my first few months at the ashram, I was confronted while 'hanging out' and talking with one of the women in my SLT group. "You're not supporting my practice of bramacharya," senior male residents said to me on several occasions. "Grow up and take responsibility for yourself," I wanted to say. As a gay man living among many hand-some, spiritual and well-built young men, I had to watch myself and temper my longing. I hadn't come to Kripalu to find a rela-tionship, though I did form crushes on several men, none of whom expressed an interest in me beyond friendship.

My coworkers and I grew close through our work together. KSS was staffed almost exclusively (except for the coordinator Varsha, a long-term resident and fervent disciple of the guru, who took the concept of selfless service to new heights) by short-term SLT-ers like me. The SLTs, as temporary residents, did much of the physical work of the ashram in exchange for room and board, while the long-term staff worked in offices or managed various departments. We were es-sentially the grunts of the Center's operation, providing an ongoing source of cheap labor while serving 15,000 guests a year.

By late May I was about to complete my initial three-month term in the program and was preparing for reentry back into the outside world. I felt lighter, both physically (only 150 pounds on my 6' frame) and emotionally. I'd broken through layers of sediment, the residue of my childhood and the lessons—intended and not—learned from family and peers. I was 35 years old, and still finding my way in the world.

One breakthrough occurred when I managed the department for ten days while Varsha was visiting her parents in the Midwest. Var-sha had asked me to take over on a day when I felt weak and raw, as if my nerve endings were exposed. I was counting down the days until I transitioned back to life in Boston while missing my friend Peter, who had left the Center a few days before. I wanted to get through my remaining shifts in the kitchen, finish my commitment to Kripalu and figure out what to do next. The LAST thing I needed was more responsibility, and yet here was Varsha telling me that she wanted to leave our department in good hands, and that mine, along with Hoback's, a young coworker, were it.

Those ten days were an eternity, as I alternated between energized pride — this was my team, and somehow I was leading them — and terror at the prospect of everything falling apart. After several days Hoback got sick and it was all on me. My coworkers were supportive but their focus varied; some took their volunteer jobs seriously while others were more interested in maintaining their raw juice fasts or flirting with the cooks than in washing the thousands of dishes that flowed through the kitchen on a daily basis.

Three or four days a week, in the midst of cleaning up after breakfast and stocking the buffet line for lunch, we had a "sharing meeting" which was facilitated by Varsha, and in her absence, by me. This particular group was willing to share deeply. In those meetings where we sat around on the carpeted floor of an upstairs room the topics ranged from sexual abuse by a babysitter to cruel taunts from a teacher — moments when we literally and figuratively held each other until the hour had passed and it was time to get back to work.

The process of managing KSS — with an insecure volunteer running the show — wasn't pretty, but the work got done. I was amazed by this taste of life outside my habitual box, and then Varsha was back. Within a few days I was exhausted and depressed, the old knot back in my gut.

Slowly, I pulled myself out of that trough, realizing that I was a not-so-young man with limited self-worth who had led a group of 10 adults, with people who had seen me vulnerable, not in control and yet they stayed in that room and actually respected me, which triggered a sense of grief for all those years lost, when I didn't like or respect myself.

I'd broken through my glass ceiling and gone beyond what I believed possible. A few days after that revelation, I asked Gary to take a walk with me up the hill behind the main building toward Monk's Pond. Then, sitting down on the grassy rise, facing the back of the kitchen where we'd worked together for the past few months, Gary looked at me and said, "You know, you have the right to take up space."

I wasn't sure if that was true. And yet in an unlikely place—a yoga ashram in the Berkshire Hills, where people chanted prayers in Sanskrit, contorted themselves into odd shapes and adopted Indian names like Snehadip and Shivanand—I felt acceptance for the man I was, along with a sense that I wasn't fundamentally alone.

After that initial stay at Kripalu I returned home, quit my job at Boston University, packed up my apartment, and put my belongings into storage. In early 1993, I returned to the ashram as a full-time resident, earning room, board and a stipend of $60 a month. I was promoted from Kitchen Support Staff to "Veggie Prep," where all the vegetables were cut and washed for the ashram kitchen. For nine more months I cut vegetables, practiced yoga, made friends and a few enemies. Eventually I decided it was time to go home, and to figure out what came next. Inevitably, those next steps pulled me back toward the Deaf Community, back to their language and their culture.

Chapter 17

Seven Stars

Soon after I left Kripalu for good and returned to Boston, I went for several psychic readings at Seven Stars Bookstore in Harvard Square. At the time, going for readings and listening to someone who claimed to commune with the dead didn't seem all that strange or exotic. My sense of what was normal had shifted beneath me during my stay at the ashram. I hadn't found any answers at Kripalu, except for a growing appreciation of the power of community and my need for more friendships in the "outside world." And though I carried a healthy skepticism about life after death and spirit worlds, I couldn't dismiss them; I'd experienced too many things that had no easy explanations at the Center, and was reminded on a daily basis of how much I didn't know.

During those first weeks back home I wondered how I could earn a living. I'd left my position as an instructor and career counselor at Boston University and didn't want to go back. So, I pulled out my copy of "What Color Is Your Parachute?" and drifted over to Seven Stars, looking for guidance. There, in the crowded bookstore above JFK Street in the Square, I inhaled the scents of incense and sage, saw pictures of angels and spirit guides, and heard the tinkle of chimes and bells, an ethereal world that felt both comforting and contrived.

One damp Saturday in February, I sat in a small room at the top of a circular stairway above the bookstore. A fortyish woman with lank dark hair spooled out my fate on a white card-table, the flick-flick of the tarot cards both reassuring and scary. But even then, I had my doubts. I'd gone to another reader a year earlier who insisted that I would meet and date "a Leo woman." When I told her that I was gay, she asked me if I was sure.

•

At some point the reader segued into a psychic reading. She told me that "a bald man who had passed on" wanted to make contact with me. No one came to mind except for Jerry, who wasn't quite bald, and whom I hadn't thought of for some time. He wanted to say hello, and that he was watching out for me, or something equally mundane.

I'd been hoping for contact with my father, who'd died six years earlier. Even then, when I was thinking about auditioning for a regional theatre in Albany, New York—my goal was to become an actor, and eventually perform with a deaf theatre company—Jerry remained on the edge of my consciousness.

I put little stock in the psychic's words or her "visit" with Jerry. But over the next several years I found myself pulled gradually, inexorably back into the Deaf world.

•

In March of 1994, just as I became interested in relearning American Sign Language by studying and socializing with deaf people, I read an article in the New York Times Sunday Magazine. "Defiantly Deaf" by Andrew Solomon, a gay man, described the culture of Deaf people, the richness of ASL, and the links between gay and deaf identities. There is a higher incidence of homo- and bisexuality in the deaf community—no one is sure why. Many of the deaf professionals I met around that time were gay or bisexual, and many hearing interpreters, particularly in Boston, were also gay or lesbian. There is homophobia in the Deaf community, but my own experiences and those of many others reflected the parallels of being deaf and being gay. M.J. Bienvenu, a deaf lesbian activist, was quoted in Solomon's article, "What we have experienced is so similar. If you are deaf, you know almost exactly what it is to be gay, and vice versa."

Though I couldn't know exactly how it felt to be deaf in a hearing world, I did know what it meant to be a gay man in a society dominated by straight men, and like most deaf people, I had to find my community beyond my family. Gradually I came to understand my unspoken connection with Jerry. Both outsiders, both different in the eyes of mainstream culture, we lived suspended between two worlds. In my uncle's case, the era he lived in and the insistence of his family and teachers that he be as much like a hearing person as possible doomed him to a life in no-man's land. If I had been born in the 1930s like Jerry, I would have faced a similar fate as a closeted gay man. Now, in the mid-1990s, things were changing.

Bill Clinton was in the White House, and government officials were no longer afraid of uttering the word 'AIDS' or of funding research to limit its spread. The new 'cocktails' were on the horizon; the disease would soon become a manageable condition rather than a death sentence. In cities like Boston, employers offered non-discrimination policies and benefits for same-sex couples. "Tales of the City," based on the eponymous books by Armistead Maupin, was broadcast on PBS, and Ellen DeGeneres's same-sex sitcom kiss was soon to follow.

Through it all there was Jerry. In the spring and summer of 1994, after I returned to the Deaf community and decided to re-learn sign language the right way, I carried my memories of him. Those memories, distant and wispy, drove me forward as I went to Club Café, a gay nightspot, on "Deaf Night" and met gay and lesbian deaf folks, our shared membership in the GLBT 'family' a point of connection. I "turned off my voice," tried to sign in ASL rather than signed in English, and met interpreters and their deaf friends.

By fall, I'd been accepted into Northeastern's two-year interpreting program, learning to translate between spoken English and ASL, while still trying to grasp the complexities of my second language. Understanding those nuances took countless hours watching videos of native "speakers" (signers) telling ASL stories, which

I translated into spoken English, and listening to audiotapes of hearing people talking about their lives, which I fumblingly rendered into sign.

I took courses in the role and ethics of interpreting, the linguistics of ASL, the dynamics of power and oppression, and the need, according to our instructors, for hearing interpreters to act as allies and advocates for their deaf consumers. I made my way through those courses with steely determination, knowing that each class would bring me closer to my goal—to work as a professional interpreter and eventually interpret for professional theater companies in Boston and beyond.

I completed my first year in orderly fashion, aware that many of the women in my classes – there were few, if any, men—signed more fluently than I did. Those young women, filled with energy and purpose, flowed between English and ASL with ease, their fluidity mocking my awkward attempts to do likewise. Still, as the months passed and I delved further into my coursework, I felt the same calling in my late 30s that I'd clung to in my early 20s, when I was training to teach deaf children.

•

Sometime later, in the winter of 1995, a roadblock was thrown in my path. My instructor, Carol, a middle-aged woman with a no-nonsense attitude, was the gatekeeper for the Interpreting Lab course, a class I would need to complete the program and prepare for my state tests. When she informed me that I "just wasn't ready and needed to wait a year," I took it as a personal rejection. Beyond my initial anger, I felt a sense of déjà vu back to my time at Northwestern, when the program in Deaf Education was pulled out from under me, when the one piece of certainty in my life was tossed away. Only 12 students were permitted to register for the lab course, and I was standing outside the gate at #13 or 14, watching my younger classmates pass me by. During that time, unsure of so much else I pressed forward, as I had when I left Northwestern for Tennessee.

Because of the shortage of trained interpreters in Boston and the high demand for their services, DEAF, Inc. an independent living center for deaf adults, started an apprenticeship program for aspiring interpreters in conjunction with a local interpreters' group. I asked Laura, one of my teachers at Northeastern and an immensely skilled 'terp,' if she would accept me as her trainee.

Laura was five years my junior, but possessed the wisdom and life experience of someone much older. Working as a full-time interpreter, raising two teenagers she had adopted as young children and teaching at Northeastern, she was a whirlwind, here, there and everywhere. Still, she retained a sense of humor and reminded me (with limited success) to give myself a break, to do my best work but not to take myself so seriously.

She took me on as an apprentice, and for the next year I followed her to board meetings, college classes, and even a doctor appointment (with the deaf patient's permission), taking notes and asking questions afterward. On several occasions, I interpreted under Laura's supervision, getting useful tips and gradually building my confidence. In the meantime, I practiced on my own, fingerspelling songs and radio news reports to improve my manual dexterity, translating English fables into American Sign Language in the bathroom mirror, even occasionally dreaming in ASL. The work was slow, painstaking, and often boring. But I persevered, and with Laura's help I gradually got better, good enough (I hoped) to pass my state tests despite my instructor's rejection.

Chapter 18

Moment of Truth

I started the morning at the massage therapist's—anything to keep my adrenalin in check. After months of waiting and reams of paperwork, I'd finally been called in for my screening interview at the Commission. If I passed the interview, I'd be eligible to take my performance tests and become a licensed interpreter in Massachusetts.

I'd been casting about for a creative outlet for years, had taken acting and improvisation classes, and interpreting seemed like a good fit. My new career choice captured people's attention; hearing people often commented on the beauty of the language. (Over time I learned not to talk about my work with the uninitiated unless I wanted to watch their painfully slow renditions of the manual alphabet).

In early 1997, after two years of study at Northeastern University, months of substitute teaching with deaf children, work in a group home for deaf adults and volunteer work at an independent living center for the deaf, I wrote a check to the Massachusetts Commission for the Deaf and Hard of Hearing and prepared for my moment of truth. Three professional interpreters would determine whether I was ready to become a professional sign language interpreter in Boston. I didn't know who would be on my panel and didn't really care; I was focused on containing my fear, of trying to think and speak clearly even while my desire to do 'the work' felt overwhelming.

I arrived at the MCDHH offices near South Station, my heart skipping beats as it often did when I was nervous. I was led into the warm-up room, a small space where one could sit quietly and think about their answers to questions about the RID (Registry of Interpreters for the Deaf) Code of Ethics, or in my case, pace nervously about the room, gaze out the window, and sweat.

I'd memorized the Code's basic tenants: maintain confidentiality in the work; use good judgment in choosing work and taking assignments; don't give advice; further one's professional skills, and several more. But the panel would want to know how I'd apply the code in real life situations—not black and white, but in shades of gray. I paced before the single window, wearing lines in the industrial carpet. I knew the Code. But could I organize my thoughts and give the panel the answers they wanted to hear?

Finally I got the summons and was ushered into another nondescript room. Directed to a chair, I faced four women who sat at a long table along one wall. I got a brief smile from Laura, a silent observer who was training to become a screener. Of the three others who would determine my fate, one was a former instructor of mine at Northeastern, a petite young woman who made up for her lack of height with a serious demeanor that said she was not to be fucked with. I'd taken her Ethics of Interpreting course, frequently disagreeing with her, and was never sure if she welcomed opposing points of view or merely tolerated them.

The second interpreter was a dark-haired woman in her forties, laid-back and quiet. The third was a legend in the interpreting community. An Amazon, she was out-sized in every way: her hoarse, raspy voice, her zaftig body, and her brash outspoken personality. Opinionated, demanding, she'd essentially gone native and married a thin, studious deaf man who seemed to be her exact opposite in physique and temperament.

I dreaded their questions. In that dread, I felt that something much bigger than my livelihood was on the line. It was the need to belong, and my fear that I'd be found wanting, unworthy of entry into the fraternity of interpreters and the Deaf Community itself.

I already knew that I, as a hearing man born to hearing parents, couldn't be a core member of the Deaf community, but I wanted to get close, to tunnel in as far as I could.

Most of the interview questions were straightforward. I knew the Code of Ethics; I gave coherent answers. The Amazon posed the only difficult question: "Suppose you were called into the ER, arriving before the deaf mother of a small boy who had been in an accident. Suppose you heard the doctor say before he left the room, 'He's going to be all right.' The doctor left and the mother approached you, frantic. What would you do?"

Technically, according to the Code, I couldn't say anything. I wasn't a doctor, had no medical expertise, and overheard something before I began to interpret.

"I'd look for the doctor or a nurse to talk with the mother. But if they weren't around, I'd tell her what I heard. After all, I'm a human being." I wasn't sure if that was the right answer, but it was the only one I could give.

I left the session drained and jumpy, wrung out from anticipation and the interview itself. A week later I received a letter telling me I'd earned a score of 87, easily passing the initial interview. In the summer, I'd take the performance tests and earn the right to work as an interpreter in Massachusetts. Each time I went in for another test, I felt panic and fear, a reminder of how desperately I wanted this credential, the approval of the State, and the validation of the Deaf Community.

Chapter 19

Changing Dreams

During my time at Kripalu, I discovered a gift for performance. In my off-hours, I worked through "The Artist's Way," Julia Cameron's book about creativity and finding one's passion in life. Since I knew sign language and wanted to try acting, I decided to combine my interests and join a deaf theatre company. Cameron stressed the power of dreams, the importance of living a creative life. I'd been featured in several skits at the ashram, performed in a resident talent show, and had carried the 'acting bug' like a virus since childhood.

But when I moved back to Boston, my doubts quickly surfaced. Was I really prepared to start over as an intern in my late 30s? Did I have the talent, persistence and drive to make it in the theatre world? Meanwhile, I found a temporary job teaching deaf highschool students in the western suburb of Newton, and began to earn a modest salary. Though I didn't want to return to teaching full time, I liked having a secure paycheck. A few weeks later, I read an article in the Boston Globe about a local woman who interpreted plays at a children's theatre and worked with a deaf boy who'd become actor in the company. If she could do it, why couldn't I?

But working as a teacher of deaf children back in Ohio, I'd acquired lots of bad habits—like signing in English-style word order and speaking while I signed—making it hard for me to sign naturally, like a deaf person. When I'd been trained as a teacher in the late 1970s, "Total Communication" was the norm. TC, as we called it, required teachers to talk and sign simultaneously. It wasn't until the mid '90s, when I began to study interpreting and advanced American Sign Language, that I learned to "turn off my voice" while signing. When speaking English, one had to sign in English word order; it was impossible to converse in English and sign ASL.

To pursue my dream of interpreting for the theatre or acting with a deaf theatre troupe I needed to relearn the language, focus on the complex grammar of ASL, and then master the interpreting process. And so in spring 1997, I found myself a staff interpreter for the theatre school at the National Theatre of the Deaf, the initial step in fulfilling my fantasy. On the first day of theatre school in May, I sat in a dusty room known as the barn on the NTD campus in Chester, Connecticut. I'd been hired as an interpreter for the six-week summer school program, though I had only a year's worth of interpreting experience. The theatre school brought together a small group of aspiring young deaf actors from around the US and from several foreign countries like Singapore and South Africa, all of whom received scholarships to come to NTD.

I thought I wanted this. During the two previous summers, I'd spent ten hectic days on a crew at an NTD-sponsored Deaf Theatre Conference in Connecticut. Deaf and hearing actors, directors, and producers came together to present staged readings of works in progress. I offered my services that first summer to learn about theatre and to improve my ASL skills. I told the staff I'd do anything in exchange for room and board.

Soon I was the "stage manager" for a new play by a distinguished deaf playwright. Distinguished, but well past his prime. Mercifully, I've forgotten the title of the play. The plot involved talking and signing animals—some deaf and some hearing, a metaphor for the Deaf and hearing worlds and how they misunderstood and talked past one another. But the point of the plot eluded the director, the cast, and me. Still, everyone liked the way I ran errands, followed directions, and relayed the director's instructions to the actors.

The next year, NTD staff asked me back and offered to provide me with room, board, and a small stipend. But this time, instead of working with the easygoing deaf man I'd been paired with the first year, I was assigned to a demanding hard-of-hearing woman who expected me to actually know something about stage management. I soon realized that crew work was stressful, a thankless task. Several months later, NTD's artistic director called to tell me he was going to be in Boston and wanted to talk with me about a job opportunity. Could I meet him for a drink the next day?

We met in the lobby of a swank downtown hotel. Mark, still boyish in his forties, smiled and said he was impressed with my energy level and work ethic during the summer conferences. Then he asked, "Would you like to become our road manager?" This involved handling logistics when the company was on tour—everything from making hotel reservations to finding restaurants to making sure all the actors were present, sober and ready for work.

I blushed, surprised that I'd made an impression in the span of two short weeks, and honored to be asked. But I'd been taking medication for depression and anxiety for years with limited results; riding herd on a bunch of temperamental actors was another stress I didn't need. I asked to become an interpreter for NTD's summer theatre school instead. After all, immersion would be the best way to really develop my interpreting skills; I'd have six weeks of intensive work, surrounded by ASL morning, noon and night.

Mark, who knew I was preparing for my Massachusetts performance tests, said he'd confer with Karen, the deaf actress who ran the program. Within a month I got the good news. I was officially on staff at NTD.

•

I spent the three-hour drive down to Connecticut listening to David Sedaris' "Naked" on cassette tape, focusing more on the pain of the author's childhood—his struggles with Tourette's Syndrome and OCD— than on the humor in his stories. I arrived in Connecticut wondering if I could hold my own with the more experienced staff interpreters and the deaf actors at NTD. My accommodations didn't help matters. Instead of the upscale inn where staff and students had stayed in previous summers, we found ourselves in a 1940's style "family camp," with facilities that hadn't been improved—or painted—since V-E Day. It was hard to imagine any families hanging out in the "rec room," which featured only a warped ping-pong table and a few chairs, or swimming in the cracked and over-chlorinated pool.

Our cabins were musty and smelled of mildew. Floors slanted, walls dripped, insects buzzed and sputtered. After finding a swarm of ants marching across the yellowed tiles of my bathroom floor, I decamped for another empty cabin built on higher, drier ground. Everything at the camp felt used up, wet, and decayed, a harbinger of things to come.

Eighteen students, several staff members, and four interpreters stood in a circle in the barn on the first day of theatre school. There were deaf and hearing actors from the National Theatre troupe and the students, who ranged in age from 22 to 39. The aspiring actors had survived a long application process, gotten recommendations, and demonstrated serious interest in pursuing a career in the theatre.

We introduced ourselves, sharing our name and name-signs, the group echoing each sign in turn. Instead of using the name-sign I'd been given years ago in Boston, a 'b' hand moving across my forehead, almost as if I were wiping my brow, I created a new sign. My curving 'b' hand traced the line of my goatee on the right side of my face—shorthand for my name, Bruce. (Name signs usually take a characteristic of a person and combine that attribute with the first letter of the first or last name, and are usually created by Deaf people). After the introductions, we whipped our name signs around the circle, first our own, then another, to see if we could catch the other players napping.

Bruce-Charlie
Charlie-Diane
Diane-Tina

The game went faster and faster, forcing players to drop out one by one until a young deaf actor was declared the winner. Everyone clapped in ASL, their hands above their heads, fingers waving like sea anemones.

Later that morning, the deaf staff and students met the hearing directors and acting teachers, the "theatre people" who'd come up from New York City to teach for the summer. I had to interpret—to voice what the deaf actors were signing for the hearing people—who stood at the back of the cavernous room. My turn came, and I focused on their flying hands and hung back, waiting for it all to make sense. I'd learned to let the message coalesce in my mind and then speak, rather than following right behind the signer and voicing each word right after it was spoken. But reading fingerspelling, trying to decipher names and places when there are no contextual cues, is extremely difficult, and I didn't know the last names or hometowns of the deaf actors.

"Louder, louder!" Lisa called out, from the back. She was an animated woman in her early 30s, the hearing child of deaf parents, and the senior interpreter for the school. Though hearing, ASL was her first language, English her second. Just as I began to interpret she took over, interrupting me. I'd clearly failed my first assignment.

On the second day, my real work began. Each of the actors had prepared a five-minute monologue for the first day of class. The director, a veteran of the New York theatre scene, needed an interpreter to translate each of the monologues, which came from a variety of plays chosen by the actors. Perched at his right ear, my job was to "voice" or speak each scene, translating the actors' signs into spoken English. Although the director knew the text, without an interpreter he'd have no idea what the deaf actors were actually signing. But I wasn't much help. I'd had only a few minutes to look over the monologues, and my dramatic background was weak; I didn't know Eugene O'Neill from Arthur Miller. Unable to follow the script and watch the actors simultaneously, I was tongue-tied, useless.

I watched Chris, a lithe 20-year-old as he signed his scene from "A Midsummer Night's Dream." Chris didn't "mouth" English words as he signed, unlike most of the deaf people I knew. I could only watch his hands. I stood to the director's right and began to translate Chris's monologue from pure ASL into spoken English. ASL word order is vastly different than that of English, and suited to a visual-spatial language. Was Chris capturing the spirit of Shakespeare's language through his signs, and facial expression? I wasn't sure; I was too busy deciphering his signs.

All I could say was: "He was driving here and there, searching and searching…for, um, somebody or something." I fumbled feverishly with the script, trying to find Chris's place in the scene. And then it occurred to me that cars were unknown in Shakespeare's time. Chris had signed, "traveling," which had morphed into driving in my pathetic translation.

Over the next few weeks my assignments changed and my load lightened. Slowly, I worked out a rhythm, responsibilities I could almost manage. I voiced for the English-style signers, who used English word order and grammar, and my partner Roseanne handled the more "strong deaf" ASL users. (Deaf people have many styles of signing, and some use more features of English, while others use pure ASL). But, in the ebb and flow of the work, I ended up interpreting for all the students -- from the easygoing Chris, who barely batted an eye when I asked him—two or three times—to repeat what he'd just said, to Steve, a heavy-set 39-year-old with glasses and a permanent smirk, who was less interested in acting than in complaining about the interpreters' sign choices, the boring teachers and the lousy accommodations back at camp.

After four weeks at the school, I received special permission to take two days off to drive up to Boston for my Massachusetts transliteration performance test. In Massachusetts, almost all requests for interpreter services were handled by the Massachusetts Commission for the Deaf and Hard of Hearing, or MCDHH. If I passed their tests I'd be eligible for freelance work, and could earn $20-25 an hour for each assignment. I'd survived the grueling 45-minute interview in the spring, and was now eligible for round two.

After months of waiting, I'd been given a mid-June date for the transliteration screening. I studied practice videotapes supplied by the Commission before I left for the theatre school. The weeks passed quickly, and soon I was on my way back to Boston. The next morning, I walked into the MCDHH offices and proceeded back to the warm up room, where I waited to be called for testing. Trying to focus on the practice tapes, voicing what the deaf folks were signing, was impossible. Instead I looked out the window and tried to slow my shallow rapid breathing.

My biggest trial was this: no one seemed to know exactly what "transliterating" meant. Everyone agreed that it involved more English-style signing, fingerspelling, and "mouthing"—silently outlining the words one was signing—than pure interpreting. But I couldn't get a clear answer as to how interpreting and transliterating really differed.

I walked into a fluorescent-lit room and faced another panel of veteran interpreters, two women and one man, fixtures of the local community. A TV/VCR combo was set up in one corner of the room, on my left. A technician popped in a tape and suddenly I was listening to the tape and signing, facing the panel members, who gazed back at me, expressionless. I began to sweat through my navy blue shirt as I signed what I was hearing, careful to use

English word order. The woman on the tape was talking about a festival, a town fair, a parade. The rest of the story has faded, the content gone five minutes after I left the room. Once I'd signed the short three-minute story, I turned toward the TV screen.

A deaf woman was signing an informational talk, "What you should know when you go into the hospital to give birth." I watched carefully, relieved to be looking at the TV rather than at the interpreters who remained seated behind me. I spoke slowly, carefully, trying to cut out my "you-knows" and "likes." Soon the tape had ended and I turned back to the judges for a post-mortem.

Their feedback was mostly positive, especially for my voiced translation of the woman's 'dos and don'ts' of going to the hospital. I'd done a good job of conveying the tone and information presented by the 'speaker' on the tape. But my transliteration of the talk on a small town parade was a bit rough, uneven. My signing was choppy and stiff, my use of space vague, unclear. One of the women, a former teacher of mine at Northeastern, said I was "working too hard" instead of signing naturally.

I thanked each of them, left the room, and took a deep breath. Then I hurried back to NTD, where I was due at work the next morning. I would have to wait several weeks to get my test results, but in my gut, I knew I'd passed.

After I returned to Boston, I received a letter confirming this. A few months later, I passed the "interpretation" portion of the test before another panel and began my brief career as a state-screened interpreter.

•

During the first week of theatre school, I socialized with the deaf and hearing actors and the other interpreters, and did my best to fit in. But the work drained me, and I spent the final weeks calling my therapist during lunch breaks, jogging around the camp to release my growing sense of anxiety, and trying to rest. (Despite my exhaustion, I couldn't calm down enough to fall asleep at a reasonable hour). I counted down the last few days, hours and minutes until I literally staggered over the finish line.

The next year, when I wasn't asked back to NTD, I felt relieved. I was chastened, too, reminded that ASL wasn't my language, and that I needed to work harder to master it. I knew, too, that I was no actor. Afraid of forgetting my lines, I couldn't let go of the script; I never got beyond my improvisation and acting classes. I gave up my dream of interpreting for theatre, too. As an interpreter, I lacked the drive necessary to prepare for one staged performance — hundreds of hours of translation working with a deaf consultant — along with memorizing the signs and structure of the play.

Underneath those logistical challenges, I also lacked the spark, the courage, and the confidence I'd seen among the deaf actors, who had voices more powerful than mine even though they didn't speak. Over the next several years, I worked as an interpreter in Boston. But once again, I found myself caught between two poles. I loved sign language and my visceral connection with deaf people. But I couldn't fully master their language and the demands of translating between two distinct worlds. After struggling to convey other people's ideas, I wanted to express my own.

•

After the nadir of my depression passed in late 1998, I began to write. Suddenly, all those years of observing others and working with various forms of language as a teacher of the deaf and an interpreter revealed something else. I discovered that I could write short nonfiction stories. And I had a particular style, which emerged naturally from my 40+ years of life experience.

Many of those first pieces focused on the shock of the aging process, of looking around and finding myself in middle age. Living with depression and anxiety, I couldn't imagine myself more than a few months into the future, and now here I was, in mid-life. Yet, on another level I felt my life was just beginning as I slowly emerged from that latest and greatest depression, the one that sent me into a hospital day program and which forced me to admit that the way I'd been living was simply not working.

It wasn't sloth that landed me in the outpatient mental health program at Beth Israel-Deaconess Hospital in Waltham, just west of Boston. Rather, it was a case of trying too hard, obsessiveness and perfectionism, of wanting to do things right and coming up short. My life as an interpreter played into my weaknesses: I worked in high pressure situations, spent far too much time alone, commuted from place to place around Boston, and struggled to understand the various signing styles of my deaf clients, who were dependent on my interpreting skills, and for whom I felt a profound sense of responsibility.

Looking around, I noticed that those interpreters who seemed to last and retain some semblance of sanity had stable personal lives — a long-term relationship, a secure place to live, a large network of friends. In the late 1990s, I had none of those things. I'd moved four times in the year leading up to my two-week stint in the day program, had a falling-out with one of my best friends, and felt worn down both physically and emotionally. I'd replaced the deep connections of living in community — first at Kripalu, and then at the Beacon Hill Friends House, a Quaker-sponsored home for 19 people on Boston's tony Beacon Hill—with life alone in a one-bedroom apartment on the far side of the city.

During my time in the Deaf Community, I noticed others who lacked those anchors. Some dove in without restraint, as if enthusiasm alone could deliver them straight into the heart of the Deaf, as if only they could make a difference. Some new interpreters went to the point of unconsciously imitating the clucking and other vocal utterances many deaf people make while signing. I'd watch them in their twenty-something fervor and look away from an uncomfortable reminder of my own need to be part of something larger than myself.

I'd always been drawn to people on the margins. In fifth grade, I became obsessed with Iceland—a stray slice of Europe floating in the North Atlantic. I read what little I could find about the island and memorized various trivia: the nation had just over 200,000 people, was the world's oldest democracy, and almost everybody was related to everyone else. Somehow my father found an Icelandic man in Cleveland, an engineer who was studying at Case-Western Reserve University, and arranged for us to visit the man's home, where we met him, his wife and his young son, all blonde and good-looking.

Throughout my youth, my enthusiasms varied with my moods and level of depression. At 16, I decided to become an actor and tried out for two school plays. Beachwood High School had a large drama department and Mr. F, the seemingly closeted gay man (though he was married to a woman) who ran the department had obvious dreams of Broadway or (at least) a professional theatre far removed from suburban Cleveland. But since he was stuck with us, he endeavored to put on high-class student productions and during that year I auditioned for two: "Guys and Dolls," and "Arsenic and Old Lace."

I was one of many in the chorus for Guys and Dolls, singing in my still high-pitched pubescent voice and dancing among a group of taller, more mature boys. In "Arsenic," I was cast as Mr. Gibbs, a small role in which I was on stage for just one scene, but which did earn some laughs. The fact that I, just over 5′ tall, was cast as a little old man did not boost my confidence.

The next year, I gave up acting for the more practical goal of becoming a teacher. Eventually I decided to teach deaf children, and began my on-again/off-again affair with American Sign Language and the folks who used it.

•

After my two-week stint in the outpatient program, I began to realize that interpreting didn't suit my personality, and my second go-round in the Deaf Community might be my last. The next summer, as I tried to figure out what came next, I took a job as a summer assistant back at the Friends' House, doing odd jobs around the old house on Beacon Hill. Around that time I got an offer to write a regular column for the weekly newspaper in Somerville, just outside of Boston.

Over the next several years, I wrote pieces for the newspaper, found a low stress job with benefits at a local college, and gradually stopped interpreting. I enrolled in a graduate program in creative writing and felt my depression slowly lift, like the morning fog over Cape Cod. I drifted away from deaf people, and gave little thought to hearing or the lack of it. Until 2006, when I suddenly lost much of my own.

Part Three
Finding Jerry and Myself

Chapter 20

Necessary Losses

In March 2006, at the end of a mild but dreary winter, I lost most of the hearing in my left ear. I didn't think much about it at the time. It was another gray late-winter morning, and I rolled out of bed groggily and answered the phone. I had to shift the receiver to my right ear; my left felt plugged up, as if I were on a plane. Days, and then weeks passed, while I waited for things to return to normal. When they didn't, I finally emailed my doctor. He suggested eardrops and nose spray, assuming (as I had) that my sinuses were simply congested.

In the meantime I had more pressing issues. I went to my dermatologist to check out a lump in my low back. The lump was nothing serious, according to the doctor. But he spotted a small mole on my chest, removed a slice and sent it out for a biopsy. A week later I discovered I had melanoma and forgot all about my hearing problem. Fortunately, the mole was caught early, and after a quick excision I was declared cancer-free.

In late summer, I finally went to an ear nose and throat specialist. Over the previous six months, I'd found it difficult to understand conversations in crowded restaurants, always a step behind, trying to fill in the gaps. Before I saw the doctor, I was given a hearing test. Sitting in a soundproof booth, I raised my hand in response to a series of beeping tones. But there were long periods of silence, while I strained to catch those faint beeps.

Glancing over at my audiogram, I knew that something was seriously wrong. The lines, which indicated my degree of loss, went straight across the lower quadrants of the graph, deep into "severe" territory. I waited impatiently for the doctor to come in and tell me how he could fix my problem. But the doctor, it turned out, had little to offer me.

"Hmm," he said. "This is unusual. You've got a unilateral loss, severe in one ear, while your other is almost normal."

"Do you know what caused it? Is there anything you can do?" I asked, my gut tightening like a vise.

The doctor was loose and relaxed. Nothing disturbed his mellow mood and his general air of disinterest.

"Nope, and not really. I'd say come back in about a year, and we'll fit you with a hearing aid."

I walked out of his office feeling dizzy, ungrounded. My ability to hear, something I'd always taken for granted, was fundamentally changed. I went to a second doctor, who was a bit more sympathetic. He explained that I had a "combined" hearing loss, most in my middle ear, and some in the inner ear. Surgery might restore some of my lost hearing, but if the surgery were unsuccessful I would become deaf in one ear. I chose the least invasive option, a hearing aid. I went to an audiologist, who fit me with one hearing aid, then another, and then a third.

The first two fit in my ear and were almost invisible, but in crowded spaces they wailed, which frustrated and embarrassed me. Eventually I settled on a behind the ear model with a visible coil, a symbol of the aging process. From time to time, I sit in the white fluorescence of her office as she adjusts my aid. I respond to a series of beeps and tones and now I can hear some—but not all—of what I've been missing.

Still, the hearing aid takes getting used to. I remove it in the rain, with wind, and at the gym. As the audiologist, a sweet-voiced Southern blonde, informed me on one visit, "Not a day will go by when you don't think about your hearing, for the rest of your life."

It turns out she was right. I worry about batteries, earwax, and losing the aid on a daily basis. I go to movies and crowded restaurants and strain to catch what I can't quite hear.

And I think of Jerry, when as a boy, I watched my uncle try to satisfy my grandfather, try to be "normal," try to be like a hearing person, but he couldn't do it, any more than I could have given up my fantasies of the high school jocks and their lean athletic bodies.

Jerry's deafness was part of him, like his funny speech, his big hands and his long fingers, which lifted me into the air when I was a small boy and squeezed a bit too hard — as if to convey the connection between us — which was unspoken because I was just a boy, and Jerry couldn't express his feelings through the strange puzzle of English.

Chapter 21

Déjà vu

It was the spring of 2007, and I was sitting in a spacious classroom at Northeastern University in Boston, back for a one-day workshop on the structure of ASL. I'd gone to NU twice, the first time in the late 1980s, when I studied higher education administration, on my way to becoming a career counselor. Later, in the mid-1990s, I returned to Northeastern to study ASL and become a sign language interpreter. After taking classes for about a year, I left the program and apprenticed myself to a working interpreter. Soon after I became a professional "terp."

I didn't last long. The long hours and irregular schedules, the stress of translating into my second language—one in which I lacked native fluency—and the isolation of doing freelance work proved too much. Not knowing what else to do, I went back to graduate school—again. I'd done quite a bit of interpreting at Lesley University, a liberal arts college in Cambridge, a stone's throw from Harvard. I enjoyed the artsy, alternative vibe on campus, and the approachable, friendly instructors whom the students addressed by their first names.

I didn't need another degree. What I did need, coming out of a serious depression the year before, was a way to structure my time and to ease the sense of isolation I'd experienced as an interpreter. And so I enrolled in Lesley's program in Interdisciplinary Studies and cobbled together a creative writing program, which allowed me to study with several writers on campus.

A few months later, I found a part-time position working as an administrative assistant for some researchers on campus. The position provided health insurance and other benefits. Meanwhile, I continued to take occasional interpreting assignments, primarily at Lesley. I'd been working with a deaf woman who was studying for her bachelor's degree for several years; I knew her signing style, her skills, her preferences. Finally she graduated and I stopped interpreting and signing altogether, intent on finishing my own degree program.

Gradually, I came to think of myself as a writer and a teacher of creative writing. Over time, my depression receded as I discovered my voice on the page. I began writing the 'Life in the Slow Lane' column in Bay Windows, Boston's gay newspaper, focusing on life outside the gay scene. Two years later, I wrote a memoir, and began to broadcast essays on National Public Radio stations around the US, including several about Uncle Jerry.

In the interim, I let go of American Sign Language. I'd always had a distinctive style of signing, my own hearing accent. Though fluent, I never embodied the natural grace of a native signer. I loved the expressiveness of ASL, and the way using my body wedded me to the message in a way spoken words did not. And yet I never got beyond a sense of self-consciousness while signing. Even in casual conversation I always tracked my progress, wondering 'Am I doing OK?' Now years after I left interpreting, I was dipping my toe back into the sea of deafness. I'd worked hard, basically learning sign language twice—the first time from hearing professors and teachers at Northwestern and Tennessee, in bastardized form; the second, years later, with more depth and meaning, from deaf instructors, mentors and friends. Now I could feel the language slipping away. Occasionally, when I ran into deaf acquaintances I found them difficult to follow, even though they adjusted their signs and slowed their pace for me.

Now it felt good to be back, to be sitting in a row of students of varying ages and skill levels. We stared intently at a tall, stocky deaf man as he lectured on the features of ASL storytelling. Bill, the professor, looked like an overgrown Iowa farm boy, with an open, expressive face that demonstrated the linguistic features he was describing.

I found his lecture easy to follow, though it was difficult to take notes, since I had to watch both his signs and his face. Fortunately, Bill had listed his topics on PowerPoint slides. If I missed a finger-spelled word, (names were particularly difficult), or if I was unsure I had caught his main points, I merely glanced toward the large screen in the front of the classroom.

Bill delivered his lecture in a signing style I absorbed natu-rally—taking up lots of space, emphasizing his points by pausing here and there, giving my out-of-practice eyes and mind a chance to catch up. He was discussing the features of "ABC stories," a com-mon form of ASL storytelling, in which a series of signs morph one into another, each using one letter of the alphabet, so that the teller quickly works his way from A to Z. Bill demonstrated a few of these stories and as I strained to catch each sign embedded in the flow, I was struck for the thousandth time by the beauty of ASL, and the natural way deaf people use it.

As Bill moved through the stories, his face flushed, his breath-ing audible, and I was reminded of another deaf teacher, back when I was a young instructor at the Ohio School for the Deaf. Ken taught my colleagues and I that American Sign Language was a full, rich language, one that took great care and practice to learn. Endless-ly patient, he put us through our paces as we practiced looking at photographs or magazine ads and then setting up the scene in "sign," shifting from one-dimensional space to 3-D, a difficult task for hearing teachers used to a linear language instead of a visual one.

I pulled my mind back to Bill's lecture in the tiered case-study room at Northeastern. Sitting in that classroom I felt a familiar tug back toward a world I'd left with few regrets. But as morning faded into afternoon, I found myself missing more of his signs. My mind felt doughy and slow, unable to absorb more information. After a while I felt lightheaded, a bit dizzy. I walked out into the chilly March air and remembered that same feeling from 8, 10, and 20 years before, when I was interpreting for deaf adults or teaching deaf children.

Each time I made my way back into the deaf world, I felt the primal need to connect to this culture to which I could never fully belong. Each time I felt exhausted from pushing myself too far. It might take three months, or five years, or in this case only one day. Still, on some level I was hooked again.

Chapter 22

Echoes in the Silence

Box Scores

Cleveland in mid-winter is cold, gray, windswept. This was not a revelation to me; I'd grown up in the suburbs east of the city in the 1960s and '70s, before global warming slightly moderated this bitter season on the shores of Lake Erie. No warming or moderation was evident on this January day as I scanned the downtown streets, looking for a place to park near the Main Library.

The city seemed deserted: few cars and fewer pedestrians on a Friday afternoon. I parked on the edge of Cleveland's Mall, a rectangular green space framed by neo-classical buildings including City Hall. Looking north, I could see the flat ice-blue lake in the background. In the foreground the Rock n' Roll Hall of Fame, the Great Lakes Science Center, and Cleveland Browns Stadium spread out along the empty lakefront.

I turned away, my neck tucked into my body like a turtle's, and pushed south toward the library. I'd spent the morning at the Cleveland Heights High School library, paging through old yearbooks and yellowed copies of the Black and Gold, the high school newspaper, searching for references to my uncle. I uncovered several mentions of a "Jinx" Cohen, the nickname I never heard when he was alive. In those old papers, I found several box scores that proved Jerry had played on both the JV and varsity squads during 1948-49, his sophomore year at Heights High. (It probably helped that my uncle turned 18 during his 10th-grade year, and was several years older than his classmates).

The Main branch of Cleveland Public Library had an archive, a collection of Cleveland's three major newspapers, two of which are now defunct—the Cleveland News and the Cleveland Press, leaving only the Plain Dealer. There was no on-line database for issues before 1990, and so I was directed into a high-ceilinged room, which housed periodicals and reels of microfilm boxed in neat rows. Scanning the shelves, I searched for fall 1948 through spring 1950, when Jerry played on the Cleveland Heights High basketball team. Sitting in that cavernous space, I squinted at the black-and-white images on the microfilm viewer, when newspapers with their screaming headlines and half-page ads served as lifelines for cities like Cleveland. I felt like a voyeur to the mid-century, almost a decade before my birth.

Looking for Jerry's name in the tiny box scores that filled the sports pages, I came across an article about celebrities who were '50' in 1951. Rudy Vallee, a star of the Roaring Twenties, was featured along with Clark Gable, and several others, now long dead and forgotten. Accompanied by the hum of the viewer, I was 50 too, searching for scraps of data about a man who never reached that milestone.

Snippets of my uncle's history spool out on screen. Like my memories of him, he is elusive, popping up here and there, sporadically. I find that Jerry played some games on the Heights High varsity team (junior varsity games were not featured; there were no box scores for JV contests). Many of those games, especially when Jerry was a junior, were losses. His point totals were unspectacular—four points here, seven there—rarely in double digits. I revise my uncle's claims of being a high school star to humble reality; he was a sixth or seventh man, a sub. Still, the box scores of forgotten games against Lakewood, Shaw and Elyria attest to the basic truth of Jerry's story—he played varsity basketball, the only deaf kid on the team, and probably in the whole Lake Erie League.

I sit in the periodicals room of the Cleveland Public Library under buzzing lights on this January day in 2008, rooting around in the detritus of my uncle's life. Maybe I have too much time on my hands. Maybe I'm avoiding doing something more productive, like examining my own past. But after this latest twist of fate—the sudden loss of hearing in my left ear two years earlier—I reflected on those other events, coincidence or not, that bound me both to Jerry and to the Deaf community he never fully embraced, a community in which I could never be a full member.

Our car accidents—he struck at 12 or 13, me on the first day of kindergarten; our experiences at A.G. Bell School in Cleveland—he as a student in the 1930s, me as a teacher in the early '80s; my 15 years of work with deaf children and adults using the language he eschewed, that he had been taught—brainwashed—to avoid; and finally, our sense of otherness in our families and in society as a whole, bound us together. Now I'm back home during a forbidding winter, trying to find Jerry once again.

I'm a middle-aged man still longing for the uncle I lost at 18, whom I knew only through brief visits at my grandparents,' when my attention was often taken up by my grandfather, and through rare one-on-one conversations when Jerry rattled on about his athletic prowess at Heights High, his life's apex. Now, as if to make up for those slights, I visit Jerry's high school and the neighborhood where he grew up, looking for a better sense of his essence and what, if anything, he left behind.

The Home Front

Like the city of Cleveland itself, my mother's old neighborhood in the inner-ring suburb of Cleveland Heights seems smaller, diminished. When Mom and Jerry were growing up in the 1940s, and during my childhood in the 1960s and '70s, the area was solidly middle-class. Today, though the houses are still maintained, the small lots are bereft of trees and shrubs and the street feels desolate under a January sky.

My mother, overwhelmed with her own life, healing from a fall and caring for her sick second husband, gives me the address and the names of the nearby cross streets, her mind elsewhere. Though I was born just a few miles from the house where my mother and Jerry grew up, the neighborhood is a warren of unfamiliar streets. I drive too far north and circle back before I find the sign, Cummings, in neat white letters.

I'd imagined the house as a boxy white colonial, like the one I lived in as a young boy before my car accident, like thousands of others built in the Eastern Suburbs just before or after World War II. But my mother's house wasn't boxy at all. Instead it reminded me of a gingerbread cottage from a fairy tale, all angled lines, shingles, and dark wood.

The house was narrow, angular, and deep, with a small porch to the left of the front door and a brick chimney that bisected the front wall, two stories and an attic or dormer in front. The chimney sectioned the house in two, along with an evergreen bush that rose as tall as the house itself, partially obscuring it from view, as if the old house were trying to hide on its narrow lot.

Though it didn't look as I'd imagined, my mother's house felt vaguely familiar. During my childhood, my mother often referred to "the house on Cummings." I imagined my uncle as a young boy, cooped up in his attic bedroom, and then later, in high school, learning to jitterbug and playing ping-pong in the unfinished basement, all arms and legs, full of the pent-up energy of the man I'd come to know.

•

Today, knowing his struggle to find a place in the family and to gain his father's love and approval, it's hard not to see the exterior gloom of that house as a reflection of the family within it—the shadow caused by Jerry's deafness—or more accurately, by Papa Ben's inability to accept it.

Chapter 23

Snapshots

Uncle Jerry smiles for the camera, holding his infant daughter and facing the photographer with his wife, celebrating his new family in a series of black-and-white photographs circa 1960. Pictured here he is long and lean, a slimmer, younger version of himself. His black hair had already retreated to his crown but his face is unlined, suffused with the false camera light and something more, like hope.

I obtained these pictures from my cousin Sue, his only child, on a visit to Dallas in early 2007. The photos were crammed into an old album and later tossed out by my Aunt Terri, Jerry's first wife and Sue's mother. My aunt, whom I last saw when I was about 10, had discarded the keepsakes of her contentious time with Jerry. The album was saved by my aunt's sister, who gave it to Sue years later.

Together, we paged through the album, fingering the faded photographs.

"I didn't know this man. I never saw him like this," my cousin said without rancor. She has few fond memories of life with Jerry. The events she could recall are painful—physical fights between her parents, screaming, bruises, welts on her mother's body. Several times she ran to a neighbor's apartment, begging for help.

The neighbors closed their doors, ignored her cries, and refused to get involved. She was five, six, eight years old.

Sue looked at the pictures and said in a tone of wonder mixed with regret, "It's nice to know they actually had some good times together."

I'd gone to Dallas to see my cousin for the first time in a decade and to probe her memories of her father, this man I knew only through the lens of our uncle/nephew relationship. Sue had last seen

Jerry when she was about 12, several years before he died, when he was granted weekly visitation.

"He didn't know how to relate to girls," she said. During those visits, Jerry took her ice-skating and sat on a bench reading the sports pages as she circled the rink. He'd smile, wave, and return to his newspaper, leaving his daughter wondering why he even bothered to visit.

The pictures tell another story, one she can't remember. In the first, Sue—about a year old—sits atop Jerry's broad shoulders. She smiles, her pudgy face framed by thick dark hair like her father's, supported by his large hands, which brace her body against him. Grabbing a fistful of Jerry's hair, she is lost in the moment, pulling with her tiny hands.

In the second, she is younger still, held close against Jerry's chest. Jerry looks left toward the unknown photographer, protective, cradling his sleepy daughter against him, her forehead to his cheek, his hands encircling her small body.

In the third, Jerry stands with Terri, she in front, he rising behind her, just to her right. Together they look to the camera's lens, to the future, which seems as bright as the glow of the camera's light. She wears a plaid jumper, Jerry a plain white T-shirt. Their faces, dark eyes and natural smiles glow with the dreams of youth.

In the fourth, Jerry sits holding another photo—himself as a young boy. I know this picture; my mother has a copy on her guest-room wall back in Cleveland. The boy in the picture is unrecognizable to me, with his longish hair, toothless smile and roundish face; he's all of two years old. My mother, big sister at four, drapes her arm around him, protective, her hair curly like Raggedy Ann's, dark in the picture, bright red in real life. They're propped on a settee, frozen in 1932. My uncle holds this picture, showing how the smiling boy had become a family man by 1960.

My cousin did not know this man, and I only saw glimpses of

Jerry's lightness, when he talked of his years at Heights High and his time on the basketball team, and when I saw him dance at my brother's bar-mitzvah. Meanwhile, the promise of his first marriage faded into anger and violence, fueled by his wife's schizophrenia and my uncle's knowledge that he would never hear, would never be "normal," and would never be enough for my grandfather.

Chapter 24

Gone Too Soon

I never knew exactly how Uncle Jerry died. I'd heard everything third-hand back in 1975—the information traveling from his flighty second wife to my grandparents, on to my mother and then to me. At the time, I heard Jerry went to Hillcrest Hospital a day before his death. He was diagnosed with the flu and told to go home and rest. (In actuality, my uncle had gone to his doctor's office a few days earlier, rather than to the hospital). By the time Jerry reached the hospital again, a day later, he was already dead. (This too, was incorrect).

The story of Jerry's death didn't quite add up. In its aftermath I was overwhelmed, not only with my parents' problems, but with the loss of my only uncle whom I loved more than I could explain. In the spring of 2007, I sifted through photocopies of his medical records from May 3, 1975. I never expected to get my uncle's hospital file. I'd heard he had been misdiagnosed or mistreated, and I thought the hospital administration might be loath to share the details with family members. Besides, my uncle died before the age of computers, and I doubted that anyone knew or cared where his paper records were located. On a whim, I called the medical records department of the hospital and explained my project to a bubbly woman with a Spanish accent. She said she would "see what I can do," and two months later I received a thick white envelope from the hospital.

In between two blank sheets of bright yellow paper were the clinical records of the last few hours of Jerry's life. The pages were Xeroxed copies, some too faint to decipher, the originals faded or smudged by years of neglect. But the sequence of events emerged in repetitive medical jargon, allowing me, finally, to piece those events together.

Examining Progress Sheets, Observation Records and Lab Reports with their orders for CBC/blood counts and cardiac enzymes, I read between the lines, wondering how this strong man had suddenly become so weak.

The first page of physician's notes, from the admitting doctor's physical examination, described my uncle as "a deaf mute," a term out of fashion by the mid-1970s; I'm surprised to see it on these hospital forms. The records referred to his wife's (Renee's) comments that Jerry had seen a doctor a day earlier, and that he'd been ill with a bad flu for the past five days, compounded by stomach cramps and back spasms. On the last day of his life, Jerry was 6'3" tall and weighed only 160 pounds. I wonder how much weight he lost in that last week, and if the flu contributed to the heart attack that eventually killed him.

The forms and nurse's notes showed that my uncle was conscious when he arrived at the hospital, at 5PM. The notes reported that the patient was "admitted directly to the CCMU [cardiac care unit]" and yet Jerry didn't reach cardiac care until about 7 PM.

As I read, images formed in my mind, moving pictures taken from my own hospital experiences. My uncle lay on a hospital gurney, eyes wide as he was wheeled from one station to another, too cold and afraid, I'd guess, to comprehend the fast moving lips of the hearing doctors and nurses or the glossy ones of his wife. Maybe he was numb, in shock. The combination of artificial light, chilled air, and the smell of the ER—ammonia, piss, blood—circled around him on this warm, humid evening, a taste of the summer to come.

By 7PM, the attending cardiologist, a Doctor Berger, took over my uncle's care. He tracked Jerry's decline, from alert to unresponsive, from weak to "expired." Only 44 years old, with no history of heart disease or other serious illness, his only previous (adult) hospitalization was in the psychiatric unit of Huron Road Hospital several years earlier, a fact that is noted in the Patient History. My uncle's only medication was 2mg of Valium—which he may have used for years, as a way of quieting the rage that seethed beneath his skin. A nurse described Jerry's extremities as "extremely cool," his facial color as "poor;" he had difficulty breathing. Additional medications---Adrenalin and Dopamine, along with oxygen to ease his labored breathing, were given in the hospital, to little effect. From 7 to about 8:20 PM, Jerry continued to decline.

What really happened in the chaos of the hospital emergency room, and later, in the cardiac care unit? One of the papers said he was "A": [alert and cooperative] at 7:20 pm, by 8:10 the column for "consciousness" was empty, and no systolic blood pressure was listed. Another paper, the Cardio-Pulmonary Resuscitation Sheet, captured my attention. The sheet was labeled 7:55 AM, but the technician or nurse surely filled out the form on the evening of May 3, 1975. The final minutes of Jerry's life are detailed as a series of Xs on the medical form. I read the notes and connected the dots, row by row.

At 7:55, Jerry went into respiratory arrest, due to "unknown causes."

A nurse recognized this, as "the patient" had no respiration or pulse.

The nurse started resuscitation within 1 minute, using a bag/endo tube.

CPR was begun by a doctor, and continued for 40 minutes.

No palpable blood pressure was recorded, no pulse or spontaneous breathing occurred. The patient reverted to cardiac standstill.

Circulation and respiration were not restored. There was no response to the procedure.

The anesthesia record states, in hurried script, "emergency intubation was done in CCU, pt's permanent bridge dislodged and given to nurse."

Anesthesia began at 8 PM, and finished at 8:10.

The cause of death is listed on the Discharge Summary as myocardial infarction—a heart attack. The words are precise, clinical, and bloodless.

"In spite of intensive supportive care the patient had a cardiac arrest from which he did not recover. He expired at 8:45 p.m. The coroner was notified and a release was obtained, although no autopsy was done."

The last form is for the release of my uncle's body to the Berkowitz-Kumin funeral home in Cleveland Heights, at 10:10 pm. By that time, I'd arrived home, and learned that Jerry was dead.

Forty years later, I still miss him.

•

I finger the smooth pages of a red scrapbook, its stiff cardboard cover embossed with a gold fleur-de-lis design, which my mother gave me a few years ago. Inside, the pages have gone yellow with age. I examine a black-and-white family photo from 1962, taken with my father's bulky Topcon camera. We're seated, my small family, lined up along two sides of Nanny Fay's finely set table, the china plates and bowls waiting to be filled with the rich foods of Passover—baked chicken, green bean casserole and matzo-ball soup.

In the photograph, my uncle sits across from me, wearing a plaid shirt. His face is blank, unreadable. Now, looking in his eyes, I see doubt, uncertainty, fear. Is this Uncle Jerry, or just my projections on a blank canvas?

•

In 1994, eight years after I left my teaching position at the Ohio School for the Deaf, I returned to the Deaf Community as an openly gay man. I'd finally accepted the desires stirred by the wrestlers of my youth. As a boy I pushed against a rising tide of feelings, and tried to bury the desire I felt but would not name. As a teenager and young adult passing as straight but knowing, on a deeper level, that I was "bent" and fundamentally different from those around me, I felt isolated, alone.

I've had the luxury of more time to find my community. Today, in my fifties, I have a group of gay friends, and live in a more enlightened era than my uncle's. If Jerry had grown up a generation later, he might have learned ASL in childhood, developed a sense of Deaf identity, have seen deaf teachers, actors, and artists, as role models. Perhaps he would have gone to college.

I've been able to continue a journey toward wholeness and to find my voice as a writer and storyteller, bringing all my identities—gay, Jewish, male, and now, as a hard of hearing man who occasionally signs—into my life and work.

My uncle never had that chance.

•

In the photograph from 1962, my grandfather sits at the head of the table at our Passover seder, a stout bottle of Manischewitz wine nearby. The photographer, my father, captures Papa as he looks up and outward with a self-satisfied smile, the king of all he surveys.

Meanwhile, I lean forward between my mother and grandmother, determined to be seen, a little boy with closely cropped hair, oval eyes and a clip-on bow tie.

Now I examine Jerry's face and feel his presence, wispy like a dream that fades in the light of morning, imagining, not for the first time, the stories we might have shared through sign language. Then I close the book, cover my uncle's face and crawl back into bed, sinking into the silence he knew so well.

Afterword

Around the time I turned 50 I conceived the idea for this book, which I came to think of as a parallel memoir, the story of my uncle and me and our brief but profound connection. A friend described our story as "an intimate relationship between two people who didn't know each other [well]," and with this project I've tried to remedy that situation, at least on my end.

Maybe writing this book was a way of taking the odd misfortune of losing my hearing and finding something positive within that experience, which felt at the time, (and still feels) like a betrayal of the body.

I celebrated the arrival of my milestone birthday with a mixture of gratitude and relief. The year before I'd weathered a series of health crises—beyond the hearing loss—with the discovery of a malignant melanoma on my chest, followed by the non-lethal but quite painful birthing of a kidney stone, and finally after the stone was pulverized, the detection of a large tumor near my other kidney. Shortly before my 50th birthday, a needle biopsy revealed the tumor as benign, and I began to think once again of Jerry, my ongoing fascination with deaf people, and the ongoing resonance between my life and his.

Taking on this project was my third go-round in deafness, though now I revisited my previous attempts with a new perspective, one informed by my own hearing loss. I sifted through the dreams of my 20s and late 30s, my failed efforts to teach deaf children and to maintain my health and balance while working as a sign language interpreter, and my revelatory summer at the National Theatre of the Deaf. Looking back, I see the evidence of my desperate need to be part of something larger than myself. And yet, it was only by letting go of interpreting and finding Jerry that I came back to deafness, and that showed me the only way of authentic connection.

As I mined my memories, interviewed family members who had grown up with Jerry, and searched for old photos and scraps he'd left behind, I wondered how much of our bond existed only in my imagination. After all, my uncle had his share of disappointments—from his two difficult marriages to his isolation as the only deaf man in his office, watching his hearing co-workers pass him by —along with the responsibilities of being a father, a husband, and of trying to satisfy his own father. Why would I, one of three sons of the sister he rarely saw, show up on his radar screen?

But in March 2007, when I visited my cousin, my uncle's only child, to interview her about life with her father, I learned that my relationship with Jerry was not one-sided.

"When we were going to Nanny Fay and Papa Ben's, my Dad always wanted to know if you were going to be there. He treated you differently than your brothers. He never asked about them."

Recently, when I asked her why, she said, "Because you made eye contact with him. You noticed him while your brothers ran off to do something else." That made sense; my brother Doug was a sulky teenager and Alex a toddler during those years when Jerry and I were together at my grandparents'.

Knowing that our bond was real and mutual drove me forward. This small book is the result.

Acknowledgements

This book is the result of a great deal of support and encouragement, which I've received over the past decade from friends and colleagues. Special thanks to my close readers, Jim Carroll, Kerrie Kemperman and Andrew Szanton, for the time and care they put into reading early drafts of my manuscript, and for their feedback.

I'm grateful for my friends, colleagues and students at GrubStreet in Boston, where I have taught for the past 12 years. I'm also indebted to my former coworkers at the Program Evaluation and Research Group at Lesley University and at Endicott College, particularly my supervisors Debra Smith and the late Susan Baker Cohen, who encouraged and supported my writing. Thanks also to friends from my various communities: Arlington Street Church, Easton Mountain, Kripalu Center for Yoga and Health, and Temple Beth Zion. Special thanks to Dave Megenhardt and Red Giant Books for bringing my publishing dream to fruition. Finally, I wish to thank Mitchell Marcus, Philip Roberts, Peter Sawchuk, and Alexander and Charlotte Leblang, along with my late brother Russell, for being present in my life.

CPSIA information can be obtained
at www.ICGtesting.com
Printed in the USA
JSHW022146060822
28994JS00003B/234